The
Communication Trench
Anecdotes & Statistics from The Great War
1914-1918

The Communication Trench

Anecdotes & Statistics from The Great War
1914-1918

By

Will R. Bird, M.M.

Corporal
42nd Canadian Infantry Battalion
(The Black Watch of Canada)
Canadian Expeditionary Force, 1916-1919

CEF BOOKS
2000

Canadian Cataloguing in Publication Data
Bird, Will R. (Will R.), 1891-1984
         The communication trench: anecdotes & statistics from the Great War, 1914-1918
Compilation of articles written 1933. First Ed.
         Published Amherst, N.S.:W.R. Bird, 1933.
ISBN 1-896979-09-2
         1. World War, 1914-1918--Campaigns--Western Front. 2. World War, 1914-1918--Canada. I. Title
D640.B51   2000 940.4'144   C00-900094-1

         Published by: CEF BOOKS
                               P.O. Box 40083
                               Ottawa, Ontario, K1V 0W8.

SEP   2 2000

This publication has been supported by the Canadian War Museum.

Also from CEF Books;
Ghosts Have Warm Hands by Will R. Bird, MM.
The Journal of Private Fraser edited by Dr. R.H. Roy.
For Freedom And Honour? By A.B. Godefroy.
Only This by J.H. Pedley, MC.
Letters of Agar Adamson edited by N.M. Christie
The Great War As I Saw It by Frederick G. Scott
Best O'Luck by Alexander McClintock, DCM.
The 50th Battalion in No Man's Land by Victor Wheeler

The *For King & Empire* series;
Volume I: *The Canadians at Ypres, 22nd-26th April 1915*
Volume II: *The Canadians on the Somme, September-November 1916*
Volume III: *The Canadians at Vimy, April 1917*
Volume IV: *The Canadians at Passchendaele, October-November 1917*
Volume V: *The Canadians at Arras and the Drocourt-Queant Line, 1918*
Volume VI: *The Canadians at the Canal-du-Nord and Cambrai, 1918*
Volume VII: *The Canadians at Amiens, August 1918*
Volume VIII   *The Canadians at Mount Sorrel, June 1916*
Volume IX: *Other Canadian Battlefields of the Great War*

Preface

In the making of these fifty-two "columns" I have used freely *Statistics of the Military Effort of the British Empire During the Great War* issued by the War Office, March, 1922; *Military Operations France and Belgium*, compiled by Brigadier-General J.E. Edmonds, various regimental histories, reports of the War Graves Commission, etc., etc. I am deeply indebted to the Librarian of the Imperial War Museum for the continual assistance he has given me on a variety of subjects, and to other officials in London who have been most courteous and kindly through all the requests I have made of them.

When *Thirteen Years After* appeared in book form a great many disgruntled veterans of the Second and Fourth Divisions wrote in and complained that I had overlooked them in my stories of raids and battle actions. So in this collection I have tried to give them satisfaction, and pray that those comrades of the First and Third Divisions will bear with me in the doing. Members of the Artillery, Motor Machine Guns, Trench Mortars, and other branches, have also written in and requested that I give stories about their doings. This I would gladly do were any records available. No doubt there is much available at Ottawa- to those inside the office-but all information there is more closely guarded than the gold of the Mint, and it is far easier to obtain a few bars of the latter than to gain access to records which should be available to any Canadian subject seriously seeking information. As conditions exist today, those interested- the men who served- will be dead and buried (many thousands are already in their graves) before these publications, promised for fifteen years, are given the public. Then who will read them?

We, the men who served, want them NOW, have wanted them for years. Any accredited person should be given access to any records in the military section at Ottawa, and all records. If he wished to write an article about cavalry, he should be further assisted. Within twenty years the veterans will have gone to their last roll-call- then they can bury for ever, with the spiders and stale tobacco, everything regarding the Great War. It will then be of no interest to the existing generations.

Many of the stories given as humourous incidents have been given me by veterans of various units, and I am most grateful for all such assistance.

Will R. Bird
Halifax, 1933

"Never was seen the like, never was heard the like, never was known the like."

Shaw

Table of Contents

Chapter 1: January 1933

January 7th, 1933

IN THE Nieppe Forest a Lewis gun was mounted on a stump and its crew stationed in a hut nearby. This was to be a protection against all enemy air craft in that region. The situation afforded much merriment to passing troops, and one morning a newly-painted sign was found beside the gun. It read:-

"All aeroplanes shot down by this gun are to be tied in bundles of ten and left at the quartermaster's store at reveille."

At Steenstraete, in Belgium, there is a fine Memorial to all victims of gas, and especially dedicated to the troops who took part in the defense of Ypres during the first gas attack on April 22nd, 1915. The inscription is in French, and reads : "On April 22,1915, the troops of the 87th Territorial Division and of the 45th Infantry were poisoned by 'the first cloud' of gas. Since then, victims of that abominable method of warfare have died every day in peace time." There is no mention whatsoever, of British or Canadian soldiers having been on the Ypres front.

Our Paddy Flynn was a most impulsive Irishman, and he was a real friend to any French madam at his billet who would give him a cup of "rale tay" instead of their eternal coffee. Such a one was at St.Hilaire, and so one morning he went indignant-ly to the Sergt.-Major and said the boys were stealing her coal.

"But have you any proof?" asked the Sergeant-Major.

"Sure I have," said Paddy. "When we came her cellar was half full up of fine coal, and now ye kin see yersilf that it's half impty."

One of the best "wiring" stories of the war rests around a young officer who signs his name "G. B. Smith." He and 16 men went out from our trenches in the Lens sector one dark night in '17. They were to repair a gap in a barrier skirting a group of cellars well in front. This officer and twelve of the party had never been out in No Man's Land before, and were very nervous as they proceeded. It was cold and frosty, and the first man near a big cavity found it by going in head first amid a mixture of old tins and wire. His rifle, steel helmet, box respirator and a coil of barbed wire got helplessly mixed, while Verey lights went up in profusion all about them. The officer, looking like an early Christian martyr, got him freed, and pro-ceeded.

Each man stepped on the heels of the man in front, clanged his steel hat with rifle muzzles, seemed to make all noise possible, but the party kept on. The officer had lost all sense of direction and was vastly relieved to come in contact with wire stakes by doubling over them. He got his men to work at once, and they toiled feverishly. Finished, in peace, they stole back to their trench after what seemed an endless journey. Next morning, looking over the way, they saw they had beautifully wired a gap in *the enemy's front barrier.*

It is quite interesting to read the list of stores left for the soldiers at Annapolis Royal for the winter of 1711. These were called *Sundry Provisions and Slop Clothing.* The provisions were 3,984 lbs. of bread, 12,435 lbs. of flour, 6,588 *messe pieces* of pork, 113 bushels of peas and 351 gallons of rumm. There is no mention of bully hardtack. The *slop clothing* was 15 *blankets, 16 pr.* shoes, 19 prs. stockings, 28 shirts, 64 watch coats, and 9 boxes *candels.* These were to supply the needs during the winter, of nearly two hundred men. Ensigns, 3s. 8d.; Sergeants, 18d.; Corporals, 12d.; Privates, termed *as Sentinells,* 8d. per day. Each man was issued with: 1 large Coat, 1 pr. Breeches, *a hatt laced,* a pair of Shoes and Buckles, 1 pr. Stockings, 2 Shirts, 2 Neckcloths,1 pr. of Gloves.

New Year's Eve, sixteen years ago, was celebrated by the 42nd Battalion in real style at the crater line on Vimy. A party of nine decided to make a call on Fritz, and chose a point between Common and Birkin Craters as their entrance. Lt. McNaughton went out first and placed a covering part of bombers about five yards from the German wire. The rest then joined him and they worked their way through the wire and into the trench. No Otto was there to greet them, and the mud was very deep and sticky, so three mounted the parapet, and others used the parados as their promenades. They reached the junction of a Communication Trench and waited there for twenty minutes before two sentries appeared. One took shelter in a corner and the other seemed a patrol. He was met by the muzzle of an army issue revolver and did a hasty *kamarad.* Then one of the men who could speak German called the other man from his corner. He came at once, then obediently dropped his rifle and reached skyward. After this ceremony the party returned to their own trenches, escorting their guests. Both were members of the 23rd (Reserve Infantry Regiment).

Our cooks tried to make a real Christmas cake when we were at Genval, the Dec. 25th after the war. It was a ponderous affair of strange colors, and stranger odors while in the process of cooking.

"You, there," said Bob Bittle, to one of the company men, his helper for the day. "Put a knife into it, and if it comes out clean the thing is cooked."

"All right," said the helper, "and if it comes out clean hadn't we ought to shove these other knives in, too?"

On October 19th, 1917, thirteen airships received orders to make a bombing raid on England. It proved an unlucky number from the start, and resulted in the famous *Silent* Air Raid. Two of the airships were unable to leave their sheds on account of cross-winds. The others went, but at the height where they would be safe from aeroplanes, encountered strong winds which were difficult to combat. One airship turned back at once. The ten kept on, but only three reached London, the others being blown from their course and dropping their bombs into fields and sea. The three at London dropped bombs in Piccadilly, Camberwell and Hither Green, destroying three buildings and killing 36, besides wounding 55. This was the sum total of damage resulting from 13 1/2 tons of bombs.

Five of the airships managed to reach Germany intact, with their crews half-frozen and exhausted. A sixth crashed on landing, so that it was completely destroyed. The one which bombed Piccadilly was shot down in France, but fired by its crew. Another was shot down and its crew seized before they could act. Still another was shot down and burst into flames, burning its entire crew. The last one came down close enough to earth to have one of its cars ripped off by a tree. Sixteen men were in the car. Some leaped as they saw what was about to happen; others were tumbled headlong or thrown from the wreckage. The airship, thus lightened, shot up again taking the remainder of the crew with it, and disappeared over the Alps, never to be seen again. Its landing was somewhere on the Mediterranean. And so the raid cost Germany five of her finest and most modern airships, and eighty highly-trained specialists of her Air Force.

January 14th, 1933

IT HAD BEEN a night of incessant, bone-chilling rain and endless mud. Our platoon had spent the hours shivering in a water-logged ditch that had been once a trench, and all were fed-up to the back teeth as we went back over the ridge from our tour in the Avion line. A new officer was in charge, a very sympathetic fellow. Our path wound past one of the craters, and the way was slippery and clogged with stray wires and debris.

"Old Bill" tripped and went head over heels slithering to the bottom of the crater. The officer hurried back and peered down into the gloom.

"I say, you poor chap," he called. "Did you fall down there?" Old Bill glared up from a wreath of old wire and broken "A"frames.

"No," he snarled in terrible tones, "I was here when this bleedin' hole *went up*."

Five men who served together in the 18th Australian Battalion met in a Sydney Police Court. The judge was an acting-captain in the unit, and the prisoner had been a most courageous soldier, but had suffered wounds so severe that he had to be sent to a mental home. It was through his affliction that he had been brought to the court. The prisoner's witness was Lt. Maxwell, V.C., who had been his platoon commander in

France. The Court Usher was Sergeant Boyce, D.C.M., M.M., and ex-Pte. Neill was the court-keeper.
Unemployed ex-service men at Melbourne, Australia, have an organization to combat criminals and those who molest lone women travellers. They provide escorts for the women, and guards for houses while people are away on holidays, receiving 1s. 6d. per week for their services.

"Nancy," a springbok, was the wartime mascot of the South African Scottish in Egypt, France and Flanders, and Pipe-Major A. Grieve tells her story in *Outspan*.
"Nancy" took her place on the march in front of the Pipe Band. Wherever she went she attracted attention, and as we paraded through the villages of France the villagers would clap their hands and call "Belle Gazelle!" Nancy soon learned to know the pipes, and if a piper in the distance happened to be tuning up his pipes she would cock-up her ears and listen attentively.
The regiment nearly lost Nancy in Egypt, but it was a call of the pipes that brought her back. At a place called Mercamatruh she broke out of camp one night. Her loss caused no little consternation among the men, some of whom believed that it was an ill-omen. In an effort to find her the pipers were spread over the desert and instructed to play their instruments. The sounds of the skirling pipes were carried across the sands and it was not long before Nancy was sighted. She ran towards the nearest piper, stopped to listen, ran and stopped again, and continued in this way until the pipers closed in on her and she was recaptured without any difficulty.

This episode reminds me of our Sandy McWhortle who was passionately fond of his beloved pipes. One afternoon we were back in billets at Nissen Huts, and Sandy was next door to us. For an hour he paced back and forth in his hut, wringing what he considered exquisite strains from his armload. Then one of the lads could stand it no longer.
"Sandy," he yelled, "for the love of Jerusalem, stop that racket."
There was a pause, then he appeared in his sock feet. "I'm sorry I didn't think o' you, lads," he said contritely, "but there'll be na mair o' the *racket*. I hae ta'en off ma *boots*."

According to figures issued by the British War Office there were in France at the close of the war the following troops:

	Officers	Other Ranks	Total
Australian	4,630	89,078	93,708
Canadian	6,241	147,587	153,828
Indian (British)	118	315	433
(Native)	31	15,578	15,609
New Zealand	1,047	24,240	25,287
South African	211	5,792	6,003
Native African	0	3,008	3,008

The Office also issued the following in connection with other ranks only:
Arms and Branches (Percentage to total of combatant forces):

	1st Sept.,1914	1st Sept., 1918
Headquarters...	-	1.68
Cavalry...	9.28	1.49
R.H. and R.F.A...	18.27	17.56
R. G. Artillery...	1.31	9.48
Royal Engineers...	5.91	11.74
Royal Flying Corps...	59	3.24
Infantry...	64.64	50.59
Army Cyclist Corps...	-	0.50
Machine Gun Corps...	-	5.66
Tank Corps...	-	0.84

THE PATROL

(by J.H. Knight-Adkin)

Five men over the parapet, with a one-star loot in charge;
Stumbling along through the litter and muck and cursing blind and large;
Hooking their gear in the clutching wire as they struggle through the gap-
For an hour's patrol in No Man's Land, and take what chance may hap.
Over the sodden parapet and through the rusty wire,
Out of touch with all good things, fellowship, light and fire;
Every clattering bully tin a Judas as we pass;
At every star shell fall to earth upon the sodden grass.
From Misery Farm to Seven Trees it's safe enough to go,
But it's belly crawl down Deadman's Ditch, half-choked with grimy snow.
Then back beside the grass-grown road- watch out- they've got it set.
To where "B" Company's listening post lies shivering in the wet.
All the dark's a mystery and every breath's a threat;
I've forgotten many a thing, but this I'll not forget-
A crawl by night in No Man's Land, with never a sight or sound,
Except the flares and rifle flash, and black death whispering round.
And I have failed at many a task, but this one thing I've learned:
It's little things make Paradise, like three hours' doss, well-earned.
A fire of coke in a battered pail, and a gulp of ration rum,
Or a gobbled meal of bully and mud, with the guns for a moment dumb.
And horror's not from the terrible things- men torn to rags by a shell,
And the whole trench swimming in blood and slush like a butcher's shop
in hell-
It's silence and night, and the smell of the dead that shake a man to the soul,
From Misery's Farm to Deadman's Ditch on a "Nil Report" patrol.
Five men back to the trench again, with a one-star loot in charge,
Stumbling over the rusty tins and cursing blind and large;

Enter the trench log up to date by a guttering candle flare;
"No report" (save that hell is dark, and we have just been there).

January 21st, 1933

THE FOLLOWING is a menu card I salvaged from a re-union of old sweats" somewhere in Blighty:

Oeufs R.F.C.
Whizz-Bangs

Creme DixMud
Consomme Water Tower

Sole Yser (bombe)

Boeuf Route Menin (Roti Hell Fire)
Yorks. and Lancs. Pudd.
Passchendaele
Sauce Glycerine
Pommes Mills
Verts Ver(e)y
Petits Shrapnel

Compote PoelcApple,
Confiture pave

Glace du Moat

Fromage Phosgene

Canal Cafe

There have been many, many cave-ins up Ypres way. A young couple engaged in love-making on one of the paths along the old ramparts were badly startled when they fell through into an old British dugout beneath. The timbering had rotted, and there were considerable cave-ins in that area. Then, on the main road from Lille to Ypres, a gigantic collapse of a German underground just east of St.Eloi caused all traffic to be sent via Wytschaete and Oostaverne. Next the Menin Road caved in fifty yards east of the old level crossing at Hell Fire Corner. This road had been tunnelled by the 14th Division in 1915. A little later there was another cave-in at the junction of Cambridge Road, where an aid post had been constructed. I was there at the time and saw the piles of equipment, rifles, blankets, stretchers, bandages, sandbags, ground sheets, etc., rotting in the depth. One could get a rifle from the heaps for five Belgian francs. Then German tunnels and galleries between Hooge and Clapham Junction caved in, and from one of the latter places I got a unique souvenir. They found the body of a German major, who had apparently been potted by one of his own gang. His only wound was a bullet hole directly under his Iron Cross, which was neatly drilled by the shot, and no weapon could be found. The diggers very kindly presented me with the drilled Cross.

The true stories of the war are stranger than any fiction. Lt. H.D. Gauld, one of the 8th Scottish Borderers, had, as his school mate at George Heriot's School in Edinburgh, Bernard von Hauenhausen, the son of a German baron, a very clever and gentlemanly fellow who carried the marks of many a duel on his body. Bernard was a "good lad" with all acquaintances and had many a banquet in his quarters, so that at last he and young Gauld were real chums.

A few years-and came the war. Lt. Gauld, on the night of August 29th, '17, was leading his platoon up to the front. There had been terrible fighting all the day, and the Highland Light Infantry had tried to capture the crest of Hill 35, which was dominated by a German pillbox. They had been swept by machine gun fire, which was uncannily accurate, until half their number were casualties.

It was a night of wind and rain and confusion. Well past midnight the Borderers staggered into the ditches that were called the front line, relieving what was left of the H.L.I. There was a sergeant in the trench who speedily became acquainted with the newcomers, saying that he was a brigade machine gunner and had a post, just in the rear. He asked many questions about the strength of the Borderers, etc., and then Lt. Gauld, who had been listening in the darkness, recognized the voice. He thrust forward.

"Hello, sergeant," he greeted. "Fancy meeting you here after all these years."

Fear filled the eyes of the man who turned as a flare flickered into the night and recognition was mutual; then was replaced by courage.

"Great cakes, old man," he answered. "We meet again under pleasant circumstances." Then he shook the offered hand in a warm grip.

"What about a shot of rum in my dugout?" asked Gauld.

"Right," said the sergeant.

Gauld led the way along the ditch to where there was a stretch without a sentry, and pointed. The sergeant turned back, too filled with emotion to speak, and shook hands again, then was gone.

As the figure of Bernard von Hauenhausen vanished in the murk, Gauld visioned all the glory, the medal, and special leave that would have been his if he had but acted only as a soldier.

For forty-eight hours the Borderers held that trench, and not one man was wounded. The murderous machine guns did not shoot near them, no sniper was active. Then the Borderers went forward to attack- and met no opposition.

The stronghold had been vacated.

It was something that the Staff behind never understood, but Gauld finally did, and his understanding urged his search to find his old chum after the war, only to learn that Bernard had died gallantly in the fighting at Rheims.

January 28th, 1933

THE BOYS of fifteen platoon had a new officer who was very nervous while we were in the old German concrete undergrounds about Cite St. Theodore. There was a dark corner where tumbled masonry blocked some sort of a tunnel, and he peered nervously into it each time he passed by, using his flashlight to do so. Then came an evening when they heard his startled gasp, and hurried retreat. He dashed back into the cellar he had occupied, seized a Mills bomb, ran forward, pulling the pin as he did so, and hurled the grenade. There was a terrific explosion among the broken concrete, a stunning report, then drifting fumes and smoke.

"I got him, boys," yelled the officer. "I couldn't miss. It was lucky, too, I was passing or he'd have got at you. He was just crawling through and I looked him right in the face."

When the smoke had cleared he used his flashlight. Shattered glass, and a mirror frame, were lying where the body should have been, and finally he understood. He was a long time forgiving the platoon.

In May, 1917, the British Army was at its greatest strength in the field, having a total, then, of 2,063,688 of infantry of the line. The average monthly strength of the Royal Flying Corps up to December, 1918, was 38,697 all ranks.

In North Russia and Vladivostock the Canadians had 1 officer and 8 other ranks killed, 3 officers and 12 other ranks wounded. The Australians had 1 officer killed. In France the Canadians had 2,884 officers and 53,491 other ranks killed in action or died of wounds; 6,343 officers and 143,369 other ranks were wounded. In France the Australians had 2,368 officers and 46,249 other ranks killed or died of wounds; 5,361 officers and 125,559 other ranks were wounded. At the Dardanelles the Australians lost 362 officers and 7,779 other ranks killed in action or died of wounds, and 639 officers and 17,261 other ranks wounded. New Zealand lost 579 officers and 12,281 other ranks killed or died in France, and 1,390 officers and 33,459 other ranks wounded. They had 116 officers and 2,585 other ranks killed or died at the Dardanelles, and 208 officers and 4,544 other ranks wounded there.

On October 25th, 1917, there were 5,097 men serving in France who had been wounded three times or more, and 34,651 who had been wounded twice. The first total was comprised of 4 Cavalry, 48 Royal Artillery, 106 Royal Engineers, 3 Royal Flying Corps, 4,797 Infantry, 2 Machine Gun Corps, 5 Army Service Corps, 10 Royal

Army Medical Corps, 99 Labour Corps, and 3 miscellaneous.

The total casualties reported in the South African Field Force from Oct. 11th, 1899, to 31st May, 1902, was 1,080 officers and 27,354 other ranks.

The sick wastage evacuated from France averaged, for the year ending 28th April, 1918, 23,420 per month.

There had been much talk in the platoon about how the women of France were forced to work. Sunday morning, in Divion, Paddy Flynn stood in the door of our billet surveying the street when two ladies met and proceeded to kiss each other.
"There ye are," said Paddy, "Two of thim wimmen doin' wan man's work."

Pratt, the stretcher bearer, once worked a month in the Medical Officer's office. He said that this is the way the different soldiers reported on sick parade.
The Irishman : "Och, doctor, I'm kilt dead in me stummick !"
The Scotchman: "Ah'm no feelin' verra weel the s'mornin'!"
The Englishman : "I don't know what's the matter-I can't eat!"
The Canadian: "I'm feeling-- rotten!"

On October 7th, 1914, at eleven o'clock in the morning, Ypres first heard the guns of the Great War, and two hours later the first shells burst in the Square. On the same day 20,000 German troops entered the town. They remained for three days, then retired in haste, never again to tread these streets except as prisoners of war. On October 13th, the first British troops received a tumultuous welcome from the citizens. Two lays later the First Battle of Ypres began. On Nov. 10th, Ypres was first bombed from the air. On Nov. 22nd, the Cloth Hall was struck by shell fire and finally was enveloped in flames and destroyed.

The military cemetery at Cambrai that was made by the Germans in 1917 to receive not only their dead but ours, centres on a great single cube of stone. On each of its faces (one broken by a British shell) is carved the same inscription- but in four languages: German, French, English and Russian. It reads thus: "The Sword Divides, the Cross Unites."

On the 6th of September, 1914, the first German patrols were in Arras, but they left within two days. The first heavy fighting in that area was at Monchy-le Preux, where the Alpine French Division checked the enemy and drove them back. On October 8th, the fighting for Lorette Ridge began, a terrific battle with cold steel in the dark, in and about the thick bush growth. By the 10th the French were firmly established on the vantage point of the slope, and never lost their grip. On Dec. 17th, they made a desperate attack on Souchez and Angres, but were turned back. At 6.30 A.M., on the 3rd of March, 1915 the Germans blew the first mines in that region, under the French lines on the Lorette Ridge.

I wonder what happened to the war souvenirs which were supposed to be sent to Canada at the close of the year 1918. According to reports read in the House of Commons on May 27th, 1919, in a speech by the Hon. Sir Edward Kemp, P.C., K.C.M.G., M.P., there were sent to Canada 107 field guns, 19 trench mortars, 248 machine guns, and 629 lighter field weapons. These may be seen at various towns and cities, in armories and parks, but what of the other articles? Article 4 of the *Memorandum on War Trophies* read: "Canadian War Trophies may be classified under three heads:-

"(a) Guns, machine guns, tanks, which were actually captured and labelled by individual Units.

"(b) Smaller articles of interest to War Museums such as German equipment, armour, shells, shell cases, munitions, etc.

"(c) War aeroplanes and aeronautical equipment."

The Memorandum was dated July 5th, 1917, and regarding the trophies under sub-head (b) said: "those which are collected by the Salvage Corps and troops generally and by the Canadian Inspector of War Trophies in the Field." Apparently some lucky Sam Browner had the cushy job of going about and selecting bombs and bayonets to go to our National Canadian War Museum. Then, in the speech, as Article 9, was read: "Trophies under sub-head (b) are being sorted in this country- meaning England, of course- at the present time, and have yet to be packed and shipped." Some of the lucky ones still had a job. Article 11 read: "The Canadian Inspector of War Trophies has collected a large number of smaller articles of interest to a Canadian War Museum, which have been taken from the battle fields where the Canadians have fought. These consist of trench signs, buried machine guns, field telephones, searchlights, rifles, etc. A special allotment of 5,000 German rifles and bayonets has also been made to Canada as well as 5,000 empty brass shell cases of various sizes. A large assortment has been obtained from the Ministry of Munitions of shells, fuses, grenades, etc., which will show the progress made in munitions inventions, etc., during the war. A varied collection of German proclamations, posters, propaganda literature, flags, German uniforms, decorations, etc., has also been collected. The total of the above results is a *very large collection* which will require a large building to accommodate them satisfactorily. Arrangements should be made in Canada for the housing of these articles before shipment, and some definite organization appointed for the handling of these articles. WHEN ALL THESE TROPHY COLLECTIONS ARE GATHERED TOGETHER CANADA WILL HAVE A DISPLAY WHICH WILL BE SECOND TO NONE IN THE BRITISH EMPIRE." --

Where did those trophies go? Where is the museum? Who was the Canadian Inspector of War Trophies? Are the Canadian war paintings in the Museum?

In the same records of that date I found interesting reference to the story of the crucified Canadian sergeant. Many of the boys believed that Story, and it became so widespread that somebody made a bronze statue representing the scene. The Germans got to know that the statue was being exhibited and sent a wireless denying that such a thing had ever happened. After receiving the wireless, efforts were made to substantiate the story and, finally, affidavits were secured from two soldiers who said they had seen the crucified man. One was said to be the holder of a Victoria Cross and the other the son of an important London official. Later investigations, however, could not prove the story and it was generally agreed that a wounded man had been left dying on a barn door beside Langemarck road, and had died on it, stiffening in death to a posture resembling crucifixion.

War Books for a Veteran's Library

Other Ranks, by W.V. Tilsley, published by Cobden-Sanderson, London, Eng. It is the best description of the front trenches in the salient that I have seen, the truest picturing of war as the man in the front line saw it. "They got back to find the Potijze pump broken. The tins and dixies were cleaned with shell hole water, then refilled at the green, scum-covered lake for tea. The cooks had gathered a bunch of broad grasses from the vinery, to give the stew a bit of body; Bradshaw wondered what they would get next to eat and drink."

Undertones of War, by Blunden. Doubleday, Doran. Is a book of vivid pictures as a young officer saw them. "It was a sparking frost-clad morning, and the guns were still. I went to see the raided post, trampled, pulverized, bloodstained, its edges slurred into the level of general wilderness. An unexploded shell lay in it, and many scraps of iron. Ponderous, frozen clods had been hurled out by the minenwerfers, which had blown enormous pits in the stony ground. Our own dead had been carried away, but just ahead were stretched two or three of the raiders. One was an officer of forty, sullen-faced, pig-nosed, scarred, and still seeming hostile. In his coat pocket were thirty or forty whistles which evidently he had meant to issue to his party before the raid. Another corpse was of a youth, fair-haired, rough-chinned. He was lying on his back in the snow, staring at the blue sky with eyes as blue and icy, and his right hand clutched the wooden handle of a bomb."

On New Year's Day, 1918, Lieutenant Leonard, of the 75th Battalion, who was on trench duty in the right area of their front line, heard a groaning out in front. He got a man with him and they went out to investigate. They found a badly wounded German on a road about twenty yards in front of their trench and brought him in. At 6.30 P.M. three men were seen near the wire, and when challenged they answered

"Patrol." The sentries in the trench were not satisfied. They fired, and the three intruders tried to escape. The 75th men leaped the parapet and captured two of them, one wounded. It transpired that they had strayed from the right flank of a raiding party 95 in strength. The unwounded Heinie was sent down to the General Officer Commanding with a card around his neck inscribed: *"To G.O.C., with compliments of Panther."*

On the 8th of January, 1918, Lts. R.G. Wilson and A.E. Burnham, and a party of 28 men of "B" Coy. of the 54th Battalion, raided the enemy's lines at 2.04 A.M. The barrage, however, had fallen short, and wily Fritz had understood what was intended and had promptly vacated his front line. The raiders could not find a single sentry, so returned, bringing with them one Maxim machine gun and one converted Lewis.

Orderly Officer: "Any complaints, men?"
Flynn: "Yis, sor. These taters is bad."
O. O. "Taters-taters ! What does he mean, Sergeant?"
Sergt. Taylor: "That's 'is hignorance, sir. 'E means spuds."

When the cooks saw Elias Greener join our ranks at St. Hilaire they were quite ready for him. He was exceedingly and very obviously new to France, and had a hungry look.
"What'll you have," asked Hooky Wright.
"Boiled beef and carrots, sausages and mash, or lamb with mint sauce?"
And Pte. Greener said: "Yes please."

When Jimmy Oller joined us the first thing we noticed was the size of his feet. He wore size elevens. That night the sergeant came to the billet and roused Old Bill. "Where's Oller?" he asked.
"Him," snorted Old Bill. "He's gone up to the crossroads to turn 'round."

Pte. Hiccup, before the Commanding Officer, when 48 hours over his leave. "It was like this, sir. The band started to play "God Save the King," at Waterloo Station, and when I stopped standin' to attention the train had gone."

Chapter 2: February 1933

February 4th, 1933

IN OUR "D" Company we had "Blackie," a swarthy, stubby, nervous, French-Canadian from the North Shore of New Brunswick. His nervousness, and dislike of officers, often prevented him from absorbing needful information. Came the big scare of March, '18. We were holding the line near Lens, and the password was introduced. It was an innovation for Blackie, and the platoon commander was apprehensive. On the first night the magic word was "potatoes." The officer spent a hectic ten minutes with Blackie, trying to impress him with the importance of challenging, then, an hour later, approached Blackie's post in order to test the little man.

"Halt!" growled Blackie in the dark. The officer halted, ,and waited, and they watched each other like strange cats.

Then the officer advanced a step. "Halt !" snapped Blackie, and the performance was repeated.

Again the officer advanced. Blackie could not stand it further. "Halt!" he yelled in tones that must have startled Heinie. "D----d you, say 'potatoes'."

Post-war amenities apparently have their limitations as the following application was unhesitatingly turned down, though it has been published in a London paper.

10 Brunnenstrasse, Gorlitz, Silesia,

The Welsh Guards, London.

It has become known to me that recruits are being enlisted for the Welsh Guards. The undersigned, a Prussian of the German nation, in his 20th year, wishes to join. I have not yet served in the Army. Thanks to my intensive, sportsmanlike activity, I feel myself perfectly sound, and am 5 ft. 10 ins. high. I am at present employed in the responsible position of optician in the optical works here. The consideration of my application is my dearest wish, and I subscribe myself,

Yours most respectfully and humbly,

Wilhelm Mayer,

Enclosure: The permission.

My son, Wilhelm Mayer, was born on 6th May, 1908, at Gorlitz, Prussia. I herewith give him my consent to journey abroad for 12 years.

.... Mayer."

Each year there is a British Christmas in France. It is for the children of the poor at Longueval, and the treat is provided by South Africans. The great South African National War Memorial is close by at Delville Wood, and T.A. Beckwith, the caretaker, is a most efficient "Pere Noel." Toys and other gifts are sent by friends in England, and the balance is made up by funds sent from South Africa.

The South African Memorial is the finest in the Somme area. It is a beautiful arc-shaped structure with pavilions at either end connected by a wall with a central-arch. Above the arch stand entwined figures representing the union of the Dutch and British in South Africa. Oaks, grown from acorns brought from Cape Colony, surround the memorial. These were reared in the nurseries of the Imperial War Graves Commission and transplanted when sturdy saplings. Some hundreds have been planted in a vista leading from the Longueval-Ginchy road to the ridge in the Wood where South Africa's men fought and died. One hundred and twenty-one officers and 3,032 other ranks went into the battle there on July 15th, 1916, and on the 21st- six days later- just 29 officers and 751 other ranks survived. Small wonder that in clearing the eleven acres required as a site for the memorial, more than 2,000 bodies were uncovered, the majority being German.

The German newspaper, *"Vorwaerts,"* gives the following figures of Germany's casualties, not generally known, under the heading, "Arithmetic of Terror."

1,808,545 German soldiers killed.
900,000 of these buried in the cemeteries of 26 different countries.
14,000 Negroes of the German Colonial Army killed.
4,247,143 German soldiers wounded.
200,000 German soldiers missing.

The newspaper states that over ten million soldiers of all nations taking part in the Great War were killed, and 9,586,000 horses suffered the same fate.

The Diary of a Tin of Bully Beef

Oct. 10. At last! Am at the front. Tomorrow I shall be in the trenches, where I expect a hearty welcome. I heard someone say: "Golly! Bully again!" Won't the chaps be pleased.

Oct. 14. Disappointed. Too many of us, so I am left behind. But Quarter says I'll be issued to new draft as iron rations.

Oct. 15. Given today to new officer who put me in his shiny new haversack. Now in the trenches. Can hear rifle being fired. Don't like Jones, my master's servant. He dropped me on the floor while looking for matches, and said "D----d that bully."

Oct.16. Jones tried to leave me behind when the company was relieved today, but my master caught him. We are now back at rest.

Oct. 18. Jones kicked me across tent three times while sweeping.

Oct.19. "Groceries " a tin can, my friend, is ill. His sugar has burst out and he has a hemorhage of Oxo. The three biscuits who have been with me are complaining of the damp weather.

Oct. 21. We are moving to the front. Jones buried the biscuits outside the tent, and "Groceries" is losing tea.

Oct. 22. Horrors! My master has been wounded, and Jones has deliberately abandoned me.

Oct. 30. The rats are awful but my armor protects me.

Nov. lst. A night of horror. Was pitched bodily through the door at a rat on the parapet. Am lying in the trench gutter.

Nov. 5. Cold, dirty, disgusted, wedged now between two sandbags.

Nov. 6. Dented on one side through being used to drive a peg.

Nov. 7. Now am a door weight. Everybody kicks me.

Nov. 10. With two bricks am supporting brazier. My solder is melting.

Nov. 12. Shell explosion has shifted dugout and all. Very much shaken.

Nov.13. The end. My corner was torn off. I see a large rat approaching...."

February 11th, 1933

Our new officer was a cheery, gallant little fellow. He came to us when we were "resting" at some dinky village beyond Bruay, and the next morning fell in a working party. We marched long kilometres before being joined by an Royal Engineer, who intimated that we were to assist with a plumbing job at a field hospital. Arrived, we saw that it had been a busy night. The huts were crowded full and the weary matron who opened the door bore traces of strenuous hours. She was dishevelled, drooping, and had plenty of evidence that she had been in contact with muddied uniforms, and her grim-set mouth proclaimed that she was feeling in battle order.

Up stepped our cheery boy. "Good morning, matron," he greeted with a grand salute. "I have come to give you a bath."

We buried him with full military honours.

Tomorrow is the anniversary of the "*Wipers Times.*" It had its beginning seventeen years ago in a casement under the old ramparts of Ypres. 100 copies were printed of that Feb. 12th, 1916, issue, and the price of each was twenty francs.

Lt.-Col. F.J. Roberts, M.C., was its originator, and Major J.H. Pearson, D.S.O., M.C., his assistant. This most popular of all war-area publications was the result of the discovery of an old printing press just off the Square in Ypres.

Paper and ink were there in plenty and the entire loot was removed to the casement. After Number 2 was published, a German "gunner" found the works with a 5.9; but another press and more type were unearthed at Hell Fire Corner. In the big drive of March, '18, the enemy captured the press then in use, together with an almost-finished edition of the "Times," only the editors escaping.

Its serials, "Shot in the Culvert," by Herlock Sholmes, "From Bugler to Brigadier," by Ruby N. Dares, and such features as "Violet's Chronicle of Fashions," "Our Special Correspondent," Mr. Teech Bomas, and "Brigade Intelligence Summary," will never be forgotten.

The advertisements were a treat.

CLOTH HALL - YPRES
This Week the Great
SILENT PERCY
Brings the House Down

A Stirring Drama Entitled
MINED
Is a Most Uplifting Performance

Messrs. Artillery & Co. present their Screamingly Funny Farce entitled
THE BLUFF
This farce promises to lighten weary hours and will probably have a long run.

The Rusty Dud, or All Is Not Dead That`s Dirty.
A picture of local interest.

Finest Orchestra Engaged, personally conducted
by O.B. Server.
Proceeds for providing Warm Woollens for War-worn Walloons.

The Poetry Column sponsored some rare gems:

"The World wasn't made in a day,
And Eve didn't ride in a bus,
But most of the earth's in a sandbag,
The rest of it's plastered on us."

"Now this 'ere war, the corp'ril said,
Has lasted long enuff.
Gorblime, said the privit with
His voice exceeding gruff,
Not "arf it ain't, and drew his face
Across his sheepskin cuff."

"Hauptmann Van Horner, in trench traverse corner,
Once heard what he thought was a 'goer,'
But he was mistaken, said Fritz Carl Von Haken,
I'll write to his widow, I know her."

And *THE AGONY COLUMN*

"Dearest, I waited two hours on the Menin Road last night and you didn't come. Can it be that a puncture delayed you? Write Cuckoo H.23. S.O.S.

FOR SALE- Cheap. Desirable Residence. Remarkable Location. Fine View. Good Shooting. Terms Unimportant. Owner going abroad on account of ill-health. Apply Fed-Up, Gordon Farm, Wipers.

WANTED- A few wire cutters. Good openings for sharp young men. Apply Box 303, No Man's Land.

Young Gentleman with University Degree (Heidelburg) would like to be taken as a boarder in an English country district. Would do agricultural work in exchange for lodging and keep. Apply Fritz Coldfoot, Lens."

And the "*Answers to Correspondents.*"
Jock (Zouave Wood). No; when on patrol work you hear "Ach Gott! ich bin gauz fed-up genwoden," issue from an unknown trench, it does not necessarily signify that you have worked too far to the left and stumbled into the French lines.
Wind-up (Hooge). Certainly not. A whizz bang does not leave the gun after it hits your trench, but just before."

Its military definitions were exquisite:
"Hooge- See Hell.
Quarter-Master- A bird of strange habits; when attacked covers itself with indents and walks backwards.
Rum- See Warrant Officers.
Fokker- Name given by all infantry officers to any aeroplane flying at a great height.
Hell-See Hooge.
Infantryman-An animal of strange habits. It displays a strange aversion to light and lives in holes in the earth during the day, coming out at night to seek whom it may devour. In color it assimilates itself to the ground in which it lives.
Area Commandant- See Dugouts.
Camouflage-From Camel and Flag, referring to device adopted by this animal of tying a flag to its tail and thus disguising itself as a ship of the desert. Hence-to deceive."

The Australians have been making many comparisons with the Canadian Corps, and these usually read so that the figures are in their favour.
416,808 Australians enlisted.
465,984 Canadians enlisted.

331,781 Australians embarked from Australia.

418,052 Canadians embarked from Canada.

60,278 Australians gave their lives for the Empire.

60,661 Canadians gave their lives for the Empire.

65 Australians won the Victoria Cross. (The "Legionary of Nov., 1929", states that a total of 62 Canadians won the Victoria Cross.)

173 officers and 3,911 other ranks- Australian were taken prisoners.

238 officers and 3,516 other ranks- Canadian were taken prisoners.

93 Canadian prisoners escaped. 526 German prisoners escaped from the United Kingdom, France and Italy. 573 British prisoners escaped from German detention, including 30 officers who escaped from Germany.

On the 16th February, 1917, 2 officers and 35 other ranks of "B" Coy., the 72nd Battalion, raided the enemy trenches in the Carency sector and captured 11 prisoners, including 2 wounded. They bombed 4 dugouts (1 with mobile charge), counted 6 dead in every trench, and trapped a working party which tried to escape into the open. The Lewis guns did great execution among them. The raiders' casualties were 3 wounded. All returned within 28 minutes. 20 electric torches were distributed among the party, and these were fixed to the muzzles of the rifles and connected to trigger guards so that they could be switched off and on easily. The faces of the raiders were blackened and white cloth patches were worn on the chest and back. The first batch of 3 prisoners reached headquarters in the Zouave Valley while the raiders were still in the enemy trenches.

The 25th "pulled off" one of the first Canadian raids on the Lens front, on Christmas Eve., '16. Capt. W.A. Cameron was in command, and an officer and 20 men from each company took part. The objective included a point in the German lines known as the "Pope's Nose," owing to a peculiar curve it had which brought it near the Canadian lines. Each party got into the enemy trench without difficulty, but two of them could not find any sentries, for Fritz had fled. But "D" Coy., under Capt. W.A. Livingstone, found their particular objective strongly manned and were able to perform brilliantly with bomb and bayonet, being careful, however, to save seven fine specimens as booty for headquarters.

February 18th, 1933

WHEN WE were out at Divion, in March, '17, there were several inspections. The chief worry of fourteen platoon on these occasions was Paddy Flynn. It had become the custom for the grand moguls to ask unexpected questions, intelligence tests, as it were, and invariably they asked them of Flynn. It was as if his honest, map-of-Ireland countenance invited them.

We had been re-organized. Platoons were now a unit in themselves, each section having its specialty, and questions in this respect were feared. The sergeant spent a morning impressing Flynn with the fact that he was a "rifleman," and made terrible threats as to what would happen should he answer differently. The inspection was on Sunday, just after church parade, and a solemn retinue passed up and down, then paused in front of Flynn.

"You," barked the mighty one, "what is your *religion?*"

Flynn rocked on his heels, his brain writhing.

"I- I'm a "Rifleman, yer Riverence," came his horrible response.

Seventeen years ago this week the terrible fighting at the Bluff began when, on Feb.15th, the enemy sprang a mine and seized the crater. The York and Lancaster Regiment counter-attacked, but, raked by fire from three sides, were simply slaughtered. An officer, writing in their regimental diary, states: "I saw the Bluff a couple of days afterward and it presented a haunting spectacle. Up on the slopes of the Crater were the dead, frozen as they had been killed, for the weather was intensely cold. Right up near the crest was a sight which drew famous generals to the place.

"Silhouetted against the sky line, and plainly visible from the British line, was the figure of the only man who had looked upon the invisible enemy. Clad in his greatcoat, his shrapnel helmet was still on his head. His right knee was bent to the ground; his right hand grasped the barrel of his rifle, the butt of which also rested on the ground. He had been frozen stiff as he died, turned into a piece of terribly arresting sculpture by frost.

"There is one curious problem connected with this affair at the Bluff. In every one of the neighbouring dugouts men were to be seen sitting in strange attitudes. They had died without wounds; but whether from the effects of concussion when the mine was sprung, or from exposure or gas, it was impossible to tell."

Several have been arguing that the raid of the 20th and 21st Battalions, on Jan. 17th, '17, was the most successful made during the war. Major G.S.S. Bowerbank, D.S.O., M.C., writes that the attacking force consisted of 800 men, half from each battalion. The raid was made in the Bully sector, and artillery demonstrations were made on either flank to deceive the enemy, the Double Crassier, to the north, being bombarded with great intensity. Three engineers were attached to each company for the purpose of demolishing dugouts and emplacements.

The raid was a complete success. So convinced was the German higher command that an attack was to be made on the Crassier that they ignored the S.O.S. of the raided lines. The Canadians had 11 other ranks killed, 1 officer and 56 men wounded. They captured 1 officer and 99 men, Silesians of the 7th Reserve Division, 1 machine gun and a few light trench mortars. Four of the wounded men died, raising the "death" list to 15. The preparatory bombardment cost one million dollars, and the raid was afterwards known as "The Million-Dollar Scrap."

On the 15th of February, 1917, the 6th Battalion, The London Regiment, raided the "Caterpillar," a strong point south of Hill 60. Colonel Mildren's force consisted of 19 officers and 640 other ranks, including 20 Sappers of the 520th Royal Engineers under an officer, and 5 men of the Australian Tunnelling Company. Six Lewis guns were taken over. A neatly-staged dummy attack was made in front of Hill 60 and a small mine fired in No Man's Land, while the Hill and the Caterpillar were smothered from sight by smoke bombs. Salvos of colored rockets gave deceptive alarm at the Bluff.

The main barrage was the work of 18 Stokes mortars, and their rain of missiles drove the German garrison to their concrete shelters, and the raiders got into the enemy trench before a single machine gun was in action against them. The biggest haul of prisoners made by any one battalion in a raid resulted, 1 officer and 117 other ranks being taken. Two heavy and 3 light machine guns were captured, and many maps and important documents secured from the German headquarters. The enemy dugouts and emplacements were then totally destroyed and great numbers of dead left among the ruins. The casualties of the raiders were 16 dead and 60 wounded.

The British Records Office states that an important figure, which they often find incorrectly stated, is the total of the British war dead, i.e., 1,104,890.

There have been arguments about capital punishment in the Army. A few figures give enlightenment. 346 death sentences were carried out.

Offence	Officers	Other Ranks	Total
Mutiny	-	3	3
Cowardice	-	18	18
Desertion	2	264	266
Murder	1	36	37
Striking or Violence	-	6	6
Disobedience	-	5	5
Sleeping on post	-	2	2
Quitting post	-	7	7
Throwing away arms	-	2	2
Totals	*3*	*343*	*346*

There are some rare bits in battalion diaries. When the 50th Battalion was in the Gavrelle sector, April, 1918, a subaltern, newly arrived with "A" Company, wired Captain Stephen, the acting Commanding Officer, that our machine guns were firing short, and asked for instructions.

The reply was one word - "Duck."

Oftentimes the Americans claim that they had a much larger war casualty list than Canada. It is not true. The Americans display the figures of 77,118 dead, but not many of them point out that only 48,909 of these were killed in action or died of wounds, which was actual fact. Nearly fifty per cent of the American dead died of disease, many in American training camps. While Canada had 51,078 killed in action or died of wounds.

February 25th, 1933

Remember the tins of condensed milk with two holes punctured by your army issue knife?

Our "Old Bill" often got in wrong with the sergeant-major. We were in the new earthy dugouts on the Mericourt front when he was called in to the S.-M.'s abode and there lectured severely. After such an occasion Bill was generally feeling murderous, but he emerged smiling. Wondering, I accosted him. "Didn't the S.M. tell you off this time, Bill?"

"Sure 'e did," came the answer. "But 'oo cares abaht that. I seen a blinkin' angleworm crawl into his tin of milk."

Many claim that the French Army was almost as large as the German force. Figures given in the German Official History of the war state that they had a total available for military service of 9,750,000, while France could only muster a total of 5,940,000.

The first use of gas shells took place at Neuve Chapelle on the 27th Oct.,1914. Three thousand 10.5 cm. shrapnel shells containing an eye and nose irritant, a "Dianisidin" salt, in addition to the bullets and burster, were tried as an experiment by the Germans. They had little effect, were not noticed by the British, as the gas was not sufficiently intensive. A lachrymatory shell was tried on Jan. 10th at Lodz, Poland.

According to Canadian reports, the venture of the 7th Canadian Battalion at La Douve River on Nov. 16th, 1915, was the first recognized raid of the war, but the 1st Worcestershires claim the honor, giving an account of a raid on Feb. 4th, 1915, at the Salient. Twenty-five raiders led by Lt. F.C. Roberts, entered the enemy trench in quest of prisoners, and though it was not a very successful enterprise, there is little doubt but what it was the first episode of its kind in the Great War.

It is interesting to read about the first experiments with bombs. The "jam pot," "Battye," and "hairbrush" varieties won first notice, and caused many casualties to both sides. When the hairbrush was being demonstrated more than forty generals and their staffs gathered to watch an expert. At the first throw only the stick went forward, the charge dropping to the ground. The majority of spectators fled, others nose-dived, some merely crouched, but no explosion resulted. After an interval a search was made, and the charge found-under the person of a general.

The Mills bombs were introduced in March, '16, and seventy-six million were used during the remainder of the war.

The "*Pow-wow*" was a weekly published in 1915 by the Public School Brigade, and contained some excellent bits. The following is one of them :

DRINK - PUPPY - DRINK

Telegram addressed to War Office by Robert Froth, proprietor of the Red Lion Hotel, Godalming :-

"6754 Pte. Thos. Atkins fainted here, after route march, at 12.50 P.M. Was brought inside, and at 1.05 recovered sufficiently to ask for brandy. Please wire permission to sell same - Froth."

War Office to Robert Froth:

"Intoxicants may only be sold to men in uniform between 12 noon and 1 P.M. War Office might consider special case. Wire immediately at whose cost brandy is to be supplied."

Robert Froth to War Office:

"Pte. Thos. Atkins.- Froth.

War Office to Robert Froth :

"6754 Pte. Thos. Atkins may receive one large brandy at own cost. Apply Home Office for permission to sell same."

Robert Froth to Home Office:

"Please wire immediately permission to sell brandy to soldier incapacitated by route march."

Home Office to Robert Froth:

"Apply War Office. Soldier may not receive intoxicants except between noon and 1 P.M.

Robert Froth to Home Office:

"Permission already obtained for soldier to receive brandy. Wire ditto for me to sell."

Home Office to Robert Froth :

"All telegrams should be prepaid. Are you prepared to pay cost of same?"

Robert Froth to Home Office:

"6754 Pte. Thos. Atkins, above-mentioned soldier, will pay,"

Home Office to Robert Froth:

"You have required permission,"

Robert Froth to Home Office:

"Too late. Atkins already dead."

Eighteen years ago tomorrow liquid fire was first used by the Germans. It was at Hooge, the famous Hooge of ill-repute. This month is also the anniversary of the first torpedoing by German submarines without warning, and the victim was the Norwegian S.S.*Belridge.* Exactly seventeen years ago Fort Douaumont was captured by the Germans.

Forty-five members of the Nursing services lost their lives through enemy action during the war.

The total percent of battle casualties suffered by the British Expeditionary Force was as follows:
France; 5 casualties to every 9 men sent out
Dardanelles; 2 casualties to every 9 men sent out.
Mesopotamia; 2 casualties to every 12 1/2 men sent out.
Salonica; 1 casualty to every 12 men sent out.
East Africa; 1 casualty to every 12 men sent out.
Egypt; 1 casualty to every 15 men sent out.
Italy; 1 casualty to every 21 men sent out.
Other Theatres; 1 casualty to every 10 1/2 men sent out.

The grand total of casualties was 11,096,338.

Scene: The orderly Room near Bruay in '17. Major Bang-Up, to "D" Company Sergt-Major. Have the men paraded and march them to the mess hut. Captain Harder is going to give them his lecture."
Lieut. Bright-Eyes, standing by. "What lecture is that, Major?"
Major Bang-Up: "The Value of Moral Character."
"D" Coy. Sergt.-Major: "Please, sir, he won't be able. He ain't sobered up yet from bein' down at Ferfay with his Jane."

Chapter 3: March 1933

March 4th, 1933

PADDY FLYNN was such a soldier on parade that each succeeding platoon commander tried to place him with company details. Once he was installed as a runner.
Left alone in company headquarters, he heard the telephone ring, and answered. The
harsh voice of the colonel came over the wire and Flynn dropped the wire and stood
to attention. There he was standing when the orderly sergeant rushed in, while the
telephone had grown red-hot.

Then Flynn was made an assistant to the cooks. Came a frightful wet and dirty
night as we moved to Passchendaele, and all the cooking staff could muster for morning was one lone match. Flynn was thoroughly impressed with its importance, so
much so that he could not sleep for thinking about it. At 1 A.M. he sat up, fished it
from his shirt pocket-and *struck it* -"to see if it was a good wan."

The grand total of British merchant vessels lost through enemy action during the war
was as follows :

Number of ships 2,479. Gross tonnage, 7,759,090. Loss of life involved, 14,287.
In addition to this 675 British fishing vessels of a gross tonnage of 71,765 were lost
through enemy action, the loss of life being 434.

Forty-eight airship raids were made on England, of which 12 included London. 59
aeroplane raids were made, and 20 included London. There were 12 bombardments
from the sea. The casualties resulting from these were:

	KILLED			INJURED		
	Men	Women	Children	Men	Women	Children
Airship raids	275	171	110	708	431	1,357
Aeroplane raids	520	195	142	1,141	585	324
Bombardments	69	45	42	210	194	634

Total killed, 1,570.   Total injured, 4,041.

According to official figures from Berlin, 720 persons were killed and 1,754 injured
in enemy aerial attacks on German territory. The damage caused by these raids was
one million, one hundred and seventy-five thousand pounds.

Many strange epistles reach the Pensions Bureau. The following are bona fide extracts from letters:

"Just a line to let you know that I am a widow and four children."

"Previous to his departure we were married to a Justice of the Piece."

"He was inducted into the surface."

"I was discharged for goitre, which was sent home on."

"Both sides of our parents are old and poor:"

"We have your letter. I am his grandfather and grandmother. He was born and brought up according to your instructions."

"Please send me a wife's form?"

"I have not heard from my husband since he was placed in a constipation camp."

TYPES IN LONDON WHO DISCUSS THE WAR

('Arry) "Ther 'bloomin' war was fought an' won by blokes like us wot come from places like Befnal Green, an' don't make no mistake abaht it. Blimey, ther old Kaiser 'ated us Foosilers worse'n all their blinkin' Guards. We showed 'em, I should fink so. . . ."

('Arriet) "Yus, we wos in ther war, we wos. Bombs droppin' all over yer. Blinkin' murderers. Baby killers" they wos- real baby killers, an' no mistake abaht it. They did kill ther poor nippers. Grub uster be hard 'cause ther separation allowance didn't go far, but I did a bit dahn Woolwich Arsenal, muckin' abaht wiv shell fuses."

(Bill, the Barman) "'Arf a pint, guv'nor? Yer know I can't say 'Okay, baby,' but I do 'comprenay-voo- papa,' mister. Yer know them French gals understood, didn't they? I never knew much abaht French, but I should worry, mister. Yer know if I could tumble to anyfink as quick as them French gals can, I'd make a blinkin' profit of meself, I would.

"Nah, I cut out all ther glory stuff- fergit it- though I did uster wonder wot we wos fightin' for- must 'ave been beer."

(Muvver) "Yer tellin' me yer've won the war `ave yer? Peace 'as come; 'as it? Yer want to do wot yer wos goin' to do when the 'war was done wiv, do yer? Well git on wiv it. I don't mind."

The old man an two boys are in Flanders, an' I'wiv 'em. I ain't 'ere at all, guv'nor. Yer think I am. Yer think you kin see me, but I ain't here, mister. I'm over there wiv the old man an' boys. Ain't it my plice?"

Many wonderful poems came out of the war, and none were finer than the lines written by Capt. Thomas Kettle just before he went into his last battle. They were addressed to his little daughter Betty- with the gift of love.

In wiser days, my darling rosebud, blown
To beauty proud, as was your mother's prime-
In that desired, delayed, incredible time,

You'll ask why I abandoned you, my own,
And the dear breast that was your baby's throne,
  To dice with Death. And, oh, they'll give you rhyme
And reason. One will call the thing sublime,

And decry it in a knowing tone.
  So here, while the mad guns curse overhead,
And tired men sigh, with mud for couch and floor,
  Know that we fools, now with the foolish Dead,
Died not for King, nor Flag, nor Emperor.
  But for a dream, born in a herdsman's shed
And for the secret scripture of the poor.

(Our Scotch Sergt-Major) "When I give the command ye are not to move until the fourth syllable of the word 'Tu-r-r-rn'"

This date is one our platoon will never forget. We moved into the line at Avion, relieving the 116th. It was wet and dark and exceedingly cold. Our rations had fallen into the mud. Drenched, starved, chilled to the bone, Old Bill got word that there was mail for him at company headquarters. He spent half the night finding the place- and received a dainty postcard, wishing him "Many Happy Returns of the Day."

On March 31st, 1917, a party of 100 of the 47th and 100 of the 50th Battalion raided the enemy lines in the Carency sector. They went over at Irish Crater to a depth of 200 yards, though No Man's Land was ploughed up with shell fire and sodden with rain, so that it was labor to move at all. They found the German Crater line flooded full with bath mats floating in the water, and the trench badly crumpled-in opposite the left, and middle of the crater line. The bodies of two Germans were found wedged in under some timbers and partly buried. The opposition encountered farther on was the 14th Bavarians. Several were killed and their shoulder straps brought back as identification. The dugouts in the second line were completely destroyed by ammonal charges.

March 1st, 1917 is a date Fourth Division men want to forget. The History of the 44th Battalion gives a pithy account of what happened. Preparations had been made for a raid on a big scale, with the use of gas, and there had been a huge amount of labor nightly in carrying in the projectors, called "rats," and getting them in place within wooden casings built into the forward walls of the trench. This is the story: On the night of the 1st, the long-awaited gas attack is launched. The nozzles of hundreds of 'rats' are opened. Along the whole Fourth Division front the deadly vapours pour across the parapet. One wave is liberated at 3 A.M., followed two hours later by a second. On the left of the Battalion front Stokes guns throw out a heavy smoke barrage. Under its cover raiding parties- 2,000 of the Eleventh and Twelfth Brigades advance to the assault on the right. The operation is a terrible failure- attended by overwhelming casualties. The uncertain wind veers and carries smoke and gas laterally down No Man's Land- over the raiding troops massed for the attack. The actual assault of the infantry goes forward in fine style, but to no avail. Battalions surge against the uncut wire and are shot to pieces. In the Eleventh Brigade, Lt.-Col. Kemball and Lt.-Col. Beckett are killed, leading their battalions. On the Tenth Brigade front the 44th and 50th send out strong parties to the enemy lines. But the failure of the gas waves has left the enemy unmolested and alert. The 44th party (50 men under Lt. Steffanson) enters the enemy trench. Meeting with strong resistance they withdrew, as directed, capturing 1 prisoner, losing 1 man killed, 2 wounded. On the front of the Eleventh and Twelfth Brigades casualties in No Man's Land are so frightful that a truce is arranged with the enemy, in order to bring in the wounded and dead."

Such is the unadorned tale of a night that almost broke the morale of the Fourth Division. Terrible mismanagement sent those most gallant fighters to their death in a hopeless mission. Such is war.

March 11th, 1933

Sometimes Billy Guild would use an affected Oxford speech when, as orderly Corporal, he visited the cook's domain. Bob Bittle, in charge, would answer him. Came a day when we were inspected by the brigade retinue and the cooks were not warned. A snooty red tab prowled to where Bob was boiling his onions and tea and what-have-you. "Haw," he squeaked, sniffing at the mixture. "Stew today, cook?"

"My dear Watson," returned Bob, from inside, "a nose by any other name could smell that treat."

Sergeant Taylor had an '18 draft to a rifle range near Ferfay. They shot at 400 yards, and missed the targets. He advanced to 300 yards, and had like results. Looking like a thunder cloud, he placed them at 200 yards, and there were no hits. Grimly he moved them to 100 yards, and not a man made an inner.

"Fix by'nets," yelled Taylor, like a hungry tiger. "Charge the targets, you blighters. It's your only 'ope."

Old Bill, worn by 36 straight months in France, neglected his rifle when we were at Bourlon, and was "on the carpet."

The O.C. looked surprised to see him, and shuffled his papers. "What was your last crime?" he asked.

"Havin' a dirty bow an' arrer, "grunted Bill.

The Captain did not like the way our Cockney answered officers, and repri-manded him. "Always say 'yes, sir,' and 'no, sir'" he finished. "Understand?"

"Righto," chirped our boy.

Sergt. W.F. Adamson of the 1st Australian Light Horse, found in August '15, at Lone Pine Gallipoli, Roman coins in a trench he was digging. They were the coins of Lucius Domitius Aurelianus, struck at Alexandria, A.D. 270. This money was used to pay Roman soldiers who were fighting the Turks un the same territory occupied by the Australians. So war goes on.

Thousands of men disappeared during the war years, says an article in the *London Daily Express*... They were never heard of again. Many were registered as prisoners of war, but prisoners' camps have long since been liquidated. Nearly 48,000 are missed by France, 8,000 by Great Britain, 5,000 by Italy, and 24,000 by Germany. German mothers have made organized attempts to learn the fate of their sons, but have had small success. In German official circles it is stated that a large portion of the missing men have married and settled down abroad, making the enemy's country their second home. Especially may it be presumed that a large number of prisoners in Siberia decided to avoid the risks of a return through Russia, and have probably mar-ried and given up all intentions of returning. There must also be a certain number who, married, have, in fear of bigamy charges, assumed other names.

Many prisoners were shot, especially outside the French camps, when trying to escape. As they removed all identification marks it is not the particular Allied Government's fault if their death could not be registered. There is a last tragic reason for the missing of many men and officers. That is the loss of memory.

Two British prisoners-of-war were set to work in a Cologne perfume factory when their German captors discovered that they had been chemists in civil life- one an Australian, the other an English major- kept their wits about them and discovered the secret of one of the famous brands of Eau de Cologne. They learned that orange blos-som was the essential element in the distillation, and decided that after the war they would start perfume making in the Australian orange country.

They now have a flourishing factory adjoining extensive orange groves, and have succeeded in producing a blend which rivals the best German product.

"My Story of the War," by a Private, has appeared in the *London Daily Mail*.

"Do that puttee up."

"Yes, Sergeant. Don't answer me back. No Sergeant. Par-r-rade S'hun. Stant-at-Ease. S'hun. Dismiss."

Your leave is cancelled. What did you say? Nothin', sergeant. Well, don't say it. Your buttons are dirty. You've got blanco on your face. Take his name.

So this is France.
Vin blanc.
Vin rouge.
Vin blanc.
It's a long, long way to Tipperary.
Stop singing.
Put that-- light out.
So this is the front line.
Look after that pretty cornflower.
Things seem very quiet here.
Is this the front trench ?
Where's the Jerries? Blam!
Where's the Jerries Things seem very, , , ,
Whe-ee-ee-eee ! Blam !
Yes, nurse. Is this Blighty?
Yes, doctor; I feel better.
Goodnight, sister.
Can I get leave?

The old village hasn't altered much, Albert.
Has she really-twins?
Had a tooth out? Who's her man now?
Yes, chum, we saw a bit of fighting.
There was a little estaminet at...

So this is civilian life-blinkin' assessments. No. OG. 1,234. Assessment, Demand, Delay, Demand, Receipt... Assessment.

Pretty hair she had, that girl at Etaples. . .
Duckboards-water rates. Funk holes-gas rates.
Enfilades-poor rates. Poplar trees-rents.
Hayloft--taxes. Sentry go-tax collectors.

Sure, it was a wonderful war. Make mine a two-decker."

"Im," said Sergt. Taylor, pointing at a very thin, white-faced newcomer. " `E ain't strong enough to carry a verbal message."

March 18th , 1933

One of our favourite platoon characters was "Russky." He claimed that his paternal grandparents were Russian and French; his maternal grandparents Irish and Cockney. He was born in New Zealand and enlisted in the U.S.A. His father was a Protestant, his mother a Catholic, so he put down his religion as "Pro. & Cat.," and blandly explained that he loved them both and wouldn't hurt the feelings of either. For a brief period Russky held a position at Brigade as a "runner." He returned with a tale of a foreign officer who appeared wearing eleven medals.

"Where did you win all those honors? asked the brigadier.

The decorated one pointed to the one first in the row. "I got dat one by meestake," he explained. "Den I got all de oders because I had dat one."

In a little room in the Prussian State Library at Berlin there are shelved, ticketed and catalogued, "ghost voices of the war." They are a set of gramaphone records preserving the wartime voice and speech of British soldier prisoners in Germany. Prof. Alois Brandl, one of the world's foremost authorities on Shakespeare, and Dr. Wilhelm Doegen, an outstanding phonetician, made them in 1916 and 1917 in order to have a record of the British ranker's speech, an intent purely scientific that produced one of the most human memorials of the war.

For two years they toured the prison camps, getting the Russian, French, Serbian and Italian speech records as well. All the British ones are the same. Each man tells in his army slang and homely idiom the story of The Prodigal Son. An identification card is attached to each record, telling the prisoner's birthplace, age and occupation as:

Born, 1891. Bolton. Cotton spinner. Very reticent.

Born, 1895. Middleton. Cotton spinner.

Born, 1896. Motherwell. Baker. Can speak French.

It moves the emotions of any listener when those mystic voices speak from the dark, barbed-wire past, and as the dialect goes on it is easy to picture the speaker and sense his feelings.

There is a restaurant in London which specializes in re-unions, and one of its most interesting assemblies is the "ex-prisoners of war" group. Lieutenant-Colonel Bond, D.S.O., who commanded the famous Kings Own Yorkshire Light Infantry in the retreat from Mons, is the chairman. Major Ward Tetley, the Army fencing champion, and Captain Gerald Crutchley, the Middlesex cricketer, are among the number, as well as Captain the Hon. Harry Bingham, who won the Victoria Cross in the Battle of Jutland. Lieutenant Wainwright is another who escaped from the Clausthal Camp disguised as the commandant, with a cushion under his coat to represent the stomach. And Captain Lucas, who in '14 led a great attack against German machine guns in the Salient. He was wounded and taken prisoner, and had to operate on himself with nail scissors in order to escape gangrene.

The Welsh National Memorial Roll of Honour at Cardiff is a book of 1,100 parchment pages, bearing the names of 35,000 Welsh soldiers and sailors who lost their lives during the war. A page is turned each day by a Welsh veteran, and this will be continued until the end of the volume.

Any Canadian in Estree-Cauchy:
   "Bong swar, Madam. Nice day, isn't it?"
   "Bonjour, Monsieur."
   "Got any doo pang?"
   "Pain? oui Monsieur."
   "How much is it?"
   "No compre, Monsieur."
   "Nor me, Madam. What a langwidge!
   "No compre."
   "Ah--combeang, Madam?"
   "On en' donne deux pour trois francs pour un trente sous, Monsieur."
   "Yes, sure it's nice weather. But, see here...."
   "No compre."
   "Combeang, then?"
   "Un franc dix sous, Monsieur.
   "Here's five francs. No change, I bet. Papeea no bon, eh?"
   "De tout mon coeur."
   "Whose a cur? What a franc and a half for a bun?"
   "Tres bonne, Monsieur."
   "No blinkin' bon at all.
   "Beaucoup monies soldats Canada."
   "Yes, I don't think, you old robber. Hul-lo Marie. Me promenade avec Madamoiselle Madam?
   "Vous dites, Monsieur."
   "I didn't, but I'd like to.
   "No compre. Qu'est ce que cela veut dire."
   "Kiss her slow, you dear, eh? You plenty kiss, Marie?"
   "No compre."
   "Got any pomme de spuds, Madam?"
   "Pomme de terre. Oui Monsieur."
   "Give us a franc's worth then. Merci dugout. Bon swar, Madam. Ta ta, Marie.

You plenty bon for me, eh?"
"Bonjour Monsieur."
"Bong dewars to you, and many of them."

Do you know what month cost the Canadians most casualties?

Ypres, April, 1915	3,958 casualties
Somme, Sept., 1916	14,706 casualties
Vimy Ridge, 1917	13,388 casualties
Hill 70, 1917	10,268 casualties
Passchendale, 1917	16,404 casualties
Amiens, 1918	24,425 casualties
Arras, 1918	16,090 casualties
Cambrai, 1918	18,172 casualties
From July 1 to Nov. 30, 1916 (Somme)	30,840 casualties
From April 9 to July 30, 1917 (Vimy)	27,415 casualties
From Sept. 20 to 31 Dec.1917 (Passchendale)	18,409 casualties
Last Hundred Days	62,632 casualties

Twenty-eight officers and 275 other ranks died as prisoners of war. 79 officers and 326 other ranks were exchanged or repatriated.

March 25th, 1933

WE HAD, for a time, a quarter bloke who was anything but popular with the boys. One night while we were at Lozinghem, our platoon sergeant had too much of the Vin sisters brew, and he encountered our pet aversion.

"I shay, you " he intoned, on the night air, "I want to tell you that you're a silly fool."

The quarter bloke comprehended the situation.

"Go away," he snapped shortly. "You're drunk."

"I knows I am," hiccoughed the sergeant, "but I'll be sober tomorrow, and you'll still be a silly old fool."

The Victoria Cross was instituted by Royal Warrant dated June 29,1856, and revised April 23 1881. The idea originated with the late Prince Consort, and it is said that he designed the medal. For all those below commissioned rank it carries an annuity of 10 Pounds Sterling per annum, and, at the Secretary of State's discretion, an additional 40 pounds may be granted as pension. On August 8,1902, King Edward sanctioned a Cross being given to relatives of soldiers who had lost their lives in winning it. This was not done before that time. The cross is made from captured cannon from the Crimean War, is worn with a red ribbon by recipients in the army, and with a blue ribbon by those in the navy.

A total of 534 had been awarded previous to the Great War. V.C.'s of the Great War were gained in these areas:

France and Belgium-	502
Gallipoli	28
Salonica	2
Mesopotamia	20
Italy	7
Egypt	14
North Russia	2
United Kingdom (air)-	1
Naval	53
East Africa -	3
Miscellaneous	2

	634

Any soldier, to his son, when asked what he did in the Great War:

Well, I learned to peel potatoes and to sling a blinkin' pick;
I learned to get a move on and I learned to make 'em click;
I learned the road to Folkestone and forgot about my home,
As I heaved my beans and bacon to the fishes and the foam.
Then the Blighty boats went by us and the harbour hove in sight,
And they disembarked and sorted us and marched us by the right.
Quick march along the cobbles, by the kids who ran along
Shouting `Apoo-Spearmin-Chokolah' through dingy old Boulogne;
And the widows and the nurses and the niggers and Chinese,
And the gangs of smiling Fritzies as pot-bellied as you please.
I learned to ride, as soldiers ride, from 'Etaps' to the line,
Days and nights in cattle trucks, packed in like droves of swine.
I learned to wash in shell holes and to shave myself in tea,
While the fragments of a mirror did a balance on my knee.
I learned to dodge the whizz-bangs and the flying lumps of lead,
To keep a foot of earth between the snipers and my head.
I learned to cook Machonochie with candles ends and string,
With `two-by-four' and sardine oil and any darned old thing.
I learned to pray for Blighty ones, and lie and squirm with fear
When Jerry started strafing and the Blighty ones went near.

That's what I did. But now, for what I never did, my son.
Well, I never kissed a French girl and I never killed a Hun.
I never used to grumble after breakfast in the line
That the eggs were cooked too lightly or the bacon cut too fine.
I never told a sergeant just exactly what I thought.
I never did a pack drill for I never once was caught.
I never played the hero or walked about the top;
I kept inside my funk hole when the shells began to drop.
So I learned to live and lump it over in that muck of war,
Where all the face of nature seemed to be a septic sore.
Where all was done in darkness and all was still in day,
Where living men were buried and the dead unburied lay;
Where endless miles of duckboards wound through endless miles of clay;
Where life was one hard labor, and the men were heard to say
That the only chance a soldier had of ever getting rest,
Was when they laid him `Westward' with a puncture in the chest.
You'd like to be a soldier and go to war some day!
By all the dead in Delville Wood, by all the nights I lay
Between our line and Fritzie's, before they got me in ;
By this old wood and leather stump, that once was flesh and skin
By all the lads who crossed with me, but never came again;
By all the prayers their mothers and their sweethearts prayed in vain;
Before the things that were those days should evermore befall,
May God, in common pity, destroy us-one and all."

There were 465,984 Canadians volunteered for service overseas. Total enlistments numbered 590,572. Of these 317,705 were Canadian-born, 150,463 were English-born, 46,850 were Scotch, 19,452 Irish. 4,730 Welsh, 37,391 U.S.-born. The remainder, 6,725, belonged to other nations. 57,833 spoke the French language.

By provinces, the enlistments were :

British Columbia	51,438
Manitoba	66,319
New Brunswick	25,864
Nova Scotia	33,342
Ontario	245,677
Quebec	82,793
Saskatchewan	37,666

Alberta and P.E.I. figures were not given to me.

Religions were given as follows:

Anglicans	186,896
Roman Catholics	33,206
Presbyterians	131,802
Methodists	83,824
Baptists	34,164
Jewish	2,574
Others	18,103

One day of crowded life in the trenches, Oppy Wood, 18, Fourth Division:

5 P.M. Arrived in trenches. Outgoing officer explains work he has done.

6.00. Note utter and complete absence of any signs of work.

6.45. Message from Battalion Headquarters. Gas signal will be two `G's' on bugle.

7.30. Message from B.H.Q. Report any qualified miner who can speak German.

7.45. Message from B.H.Q. Gas signal will be two blasts of a whistle.

8.00. Message from B.H.Q. A French aeroplane with appearance of being a German in your locality.

9.00. Message from B.H.Q. For word 'French' read `German' and ditto.

11.00. Message from B.H.Q. Gas signal will be two beats on a shell gong.

1.30. A.M. Message from B.H.Q. C.O. suggests you dig out Bean Sap.

2.40. Message from B.H.Q, Find date of issue of all gas helmets.

3.20. Message from B.H.Q. Cancel working party at Bean Sap.

6.30. Message from B.H.Q. Men in trenches are not to shoot at aeroplanes.

10.00. Message from B.H.Q. Request re-bury German at Bean Sap.

2.00. Message from B.H.Q. Fill in all workings at Bean Sap.

5.00. Message from B.H.Q. Carry on with usual night work."

War Books for a Veteran's Library

Her Privates We, by Davies, London. A most striking war story by a Welsh private. One of the most sincere accounts of a soldier's emotions that I have read. ". . the air was alive with the rush and flutter of wings; it was ripped by screaming shells, hissing like tons of molten metal plunged suddenly into water... shells that were like hell-cats humped and spitting, little sounds, unpleasantly close, like the plucking of tense strings, and something tangling his feet, tearing at his trousers and puttees as he stumbled over it, and then a face suddenly, an inconceivably distorted face, which raved and sobbed at him as he fell with it into a shell hole."

Was It Yesterday? by Major Bowen, the finest story of the eighteen- pounders that I have seen. The account of the writer's experiences in Souchez Valley, and his patrol on the crater line at Vimy, is priceless.

As German translations, I have *Zero Hour*, by Georg Grabenhorst; *The Storm of Steel, by* Junger; *Private Suhren*, by Georg von der Vring; *The Fiery Way*, by Franz Schauwecker; ;*War*, by Ludwig Renn; *A Fatalist At War*, by Rudolf Binding; and, poorest of all, I think, *All Quiet On The Western Front*. Junger's book is easily the best, Renn's next, and Binding's third. These, and, possibly *Zero Hour*, should be had to obtain a clear view of the German mind displayed in such writings. They give the impression that their stick bombs were frightful instruments of war, deadly and discouraging to the British troops, while the Mills grenade is almost disregarded. When one remembers actual cases it makes him wonder whether the German intellect is twisted or not in its adoration of the Fatherland and all pertaining thereto. And, as natural as water flowing downhill, they record the endless triumphs of all their main characters, and the rotten luck against them when they were at last compelled to give way before overwhelming numbers. The naive manner in which even Junger records constant superiority whenever the British are encountered only engenders merriment to the veteran reader; there can be no bitterness; the writer is too much in earnest to be loosing animosity.

I Escape, by Capt. J.L. Hardy, is very interesting, and describes in detail the surroundings of the average German prison camp. *Unknown Warriors*, by K. E. *Luard*, is a splendid account of the dressing stations and field hospitals. *The Mud Larks*, by Garstin, brings back all the humor of the front. And if you want thought-provoking stories, intense, packed with feelings, read and own, *The Bitter End*, by Brophy; *The Somme*, by A.D. Griestwood; *Memoirs of An Infantry Officer*, by Sassoon; *The Jesting Army*, by Raymond; *Goodbye To All That*, by Robert Graves; *War Letters to A Wife*, by Fielding; *War, Wine and Women*, by Wilfrid Saint-Mande, is another book that should be on the veteran's shelf. *Lives of a Bengal Lancer*, by Yeats-Brown, another.

Chapter 4: April 1933

April 1st, 1933

IN THOSE last chilling, sloppy days of March, '17, a draft came to us at Dumbell Camp, and with them was the most doleful, cheerless young man I saw in the army. He was so dispirited that he never tried for an extra issue of hot tea, or cared where he slept. The sergeant, after vain attempts at rousing him, told our officer about him, and that worthy came in the morning as the dismal lad sat outside his crowded bivvy in a fine drizzle.

"Come, come, my boy, said the officer after several fruitless attempts to gain interest, "Tell me what you were before you enlisted?"

The boy raised slowly his saddened features.

"I was 'appy sir," he croaked.

The proportion of letter to parcel bags delivered in France was about 2 to 5. In one week in December, 1915, 5,160,713 letters and 52,477 parcels were delivered. In the week of Christmas, 1916, 123,342 bags of mail were delivered, and these figures were only surpassed in the Christmas week of '18, when 171,840 bags of mail were delivered.

In December, '14, a postal truck containing 50 bags of mail were burned in a railway collision. In January, '16, a field post office at Sauzanne, on the Somme, was destroyed by shell fire. In March '16, 37 bags of mail were lost when the steamer *Sussex* was torpedoed. In June, '16, a mail lorry, loaded heavily, was struck by a shell outside the army post office near Poperinghe, and set on fire. In August, '16, 26 bags of mail were lost in a railway accident. In November, '17, the enemy made a surprise attack and captured all the mail of the 6th Division at Gouzeaucourt. Beside these instances, mail was lost in another railway accident, and six other times by enemy action.

Seventeen years ago the Canadian Second Division endured an inferno of mud and death and mistakes at St.Eloi. The area had been the scene of mining and counter-mining during 1915. The British fired 13 mines and 29 camouflets, the Germans 20 mines and 2 camouflets. The main object was "the mound," 30 feet in height and half an acre in extent, situated inside the German lines. Six mines were prepared early in '16, containing, respectively, 1,800 lbs., 31,000 lbs.,15,000 lbs., 13,500 lbs., 12,000 lbs., and 600 lbs. of ammonal. The Germans overheard a telephone conversation dealing with the mines, and sent their experts to make investigations. These reported "no mining." The attack was made by British troops on March 27th. One battalion reached the enemy trench with only one casualty; others lost heavily. 201 prisoners were captured.

It rained heavily, and the cratered ground was a morass, so changed by the new craters as to be unrecognizable. The first Canadians in the line were a company of the 18th Battalion. The Germans had reached the craters, due to confusion of the attackers, and held on until April 3rd, when the last garrison, in Crater 5, 5 officers and 77 men, - three days without food - surrendered. The British now held the ground that had been "the Mound". Wearing steel helmets for the first time - fifty per company - the Canadian Sixth Brigade took over the new line before it had been consolidated. The 27th and 31st took over, and captured 3 Germans in Craters 5 and 6. It was a terrible area. The trenches were undrained ditches; there were no Communication Trenches; the shelters were water-logged; wounded and dead were half-buried in the mud. The Germans attacked at 8 A.M. on the 6th, and secured Craters 2, 3, 4 and 5. The 31st held Crater 6. There were 17 mine craters in their immediate area. It rained continually, and the Canadians were new to the front. They got completely mistaken about the craters held, gave wrong reports, had wrong artillery shoots. It was 25 acres of hell on earth, and the Canadians earned a thousand Victoria Crosses in the fighting that lasted three weeks. The Second Division lost 36 officers and 1,337 other ranks in that time. The German account says they lost in the initial attack 107 killed, 267 wounded, and 547 missing in the fighting; against the Canadians, who suffered 66 killed, 299 wounded and 118 missing. The "Mound", now Crater 3, remained in the hands of the enemy.

"Broncho Bill" was the outstanding deserter of the war. He was an Australian outlaw from the Back Blocks, doing five years' penal servitude, released in Sept., 1914, so that he may join the Australian contingent. He was a splendid soldier in the line; out of it, he resented discipline. At Reninghelst, he deserted. He broke into an officers' quarters, stole a uniform and several subalterns' chit books. By means of forged signatures and using the books, he won himself substantial sums at various paymasters' offices. Others of his
ilk joined him, and they had a grand time spending the money, but all except Bill were arrested. He was not caught, and he always evaded all search. Later, an escort of police, under a sergeant, presented themselves at the prisoners' cage, armed with an order for their conveyance to a trial by court martial. The prisoners were handed over; the sergeant was Bill, and his force, new-found cronies.

An informer sent word that Bill and his mates were in a certain town where there had been many robberies. The town was surrounded and the Assistant Provost Marshal motored in to effect the capture. His car was met by a squad of police who saluted smartly - Bill and his fellows. They helped form the cordon until the thrill waned, when they departed. He rejoined the Australians and again was outstanding in his front line performances, but at Neuve Eglise started a game of "One Up," using coins with two heads. In two nights he won 700 francs, then his fraud was exposed. He escaped by covering his retreat with a revolver. He was trailed to a dugout at Dickebusch, and there trapped with two others. Next morning he knocked down his sentry, seized his rifle and decamped. Both his comrades were re-captured, but Bill escaped, stole an officer's horse at Brigade headquarters, and left the area. In '18 he was back with the Aussies doing magnificent fighting, then vanished and was not seen again.

April 8th, 1933

NINE WEARISOME nights in succession we had been doing carrying parties along Cow Trench at Lieven. Snooty lance-jacks from the Engineers directed the moving of endless "A" frames, barbed wire and corrugated iron. They, themselves, seemed immune from all labor. On the tenth night we were in supports, and Paddy Flynn was stationed as sentry in the trench. Someone advanced in the dark. "Halt," ordered Paddy. "Who goes there?"

"One of the Engineers," came the answer. Paddy peered into the murk. "Yer a liar," he flung baek. "Yer carryin' something."

Do you know that there are 923 British War Cemeteries resulting from the Great War?

That Terlincthun Cemetery at Wimille contains the graves of 2,551 Britishers, 277 Canadians, 88 Australians, 29 New Zealanders, 10 Newfoundlanders, 1 Guernsey, 34 South Africans, 5 British West Indies, 1 American, 27 Italians; 4 Russians, 3 Poles, 2 Serbians,188 Germans, and 16 "Known Unto God?"

That there are Germans buried in nearly fifty per cent of the Cemeteries, and French and Belgians? That at Locre No.10 there are 95 more German graves than any others? Les Baraques Cemetery has 1,002 Britishers, 27 Australians, 25 Canadians, 16 South Africans, 7 Indians, 4 New Zealanders, 1 Newfoundlander, 1 Guernsey, 1 British West Indies, 1 Fiji Islander, 17 Egyptians, 203 Chinese, 28 Americans, 26 Portuguese,1 Belgian, 1 Japanese, 236 Germans, 15 "Known Unto God?"

Thirty-two Cemeteries have just one Canadian grave. Four have more than 1,000 Canadian graves. Wimereux Cemetery has a Memorial Seat to Lieutenant-Colonel John McCrae. There are more Canadian graves at Etaples than in any other cemetery. At Railway Dugouts, near Ypres there are 332 special memorials in the cemetery. Toronto Avenue Cemetery has only Australian graves. Noyelles-sur-mer Cemetery contains only Chinese graves. It is entirely Chinese work, even to the modelling of the stones. Ninth Avenue Cemetery contains but one large grave. In it are buried 1 officer and 41 men of the lst Cameron Highlanders.

Did you know that 50 Canadians are buried in Zivy Crater, and 52 in Lichfield Crater, at Vimy?

That three of the British War Cemeteries are entirely the graves of prisoners of war who died after being captured?

That there are only three Cemeteries entirely Canadian, and none have Canadian names? They are Givenchy Road, Mill Switch, and St. Olle. At St. Olle there are just 97 graves, and 73 of them are of the 116th Battalion.

Guards Graves Cemetery is in a forest, one long sunken trench, one of the most beautiful and unique grounds in France. 98 Guardsmen are sleeping there. Many of the cemeteries have unlovely names, such as Mud Corner, Bulls Road, Rookery, Thistle Dump, Crump Trench, Cuckoo Passage, Beehive and Sand Pits.

After the ground had been thoroughly searched on three separate occasions, two "lost" war cemeteries were found near Sanctuary Wood in 1928. In April of that year 80 bodies were recovered in what was a part of Baron de Vinck's grounds, he of the famous Hooge Chateau. These had been buried in 1915. The other was a 1916 cemetery, and 82 bodies were recovered from it, many of them buried nine feet below the surface. Only one man was identified, though badges established the units of nearly all. Every man had been buried at leisure, as all pockets had been searched, identity disks and pay books removed. These bodies were in a remarkable state of preservation when brought to the surface, and anyone who had known them in life could have identified them easily.

The following statistics have been compiled by Christie Street Hospital Branch of the Canadian Legion: In Canada prior to the war, were 2,410,649 males between 18 and 45 years old.

Total Number enlisted in Canadian Expeditionary Force, 619,636,
Total who served outside of Canada, 424,589.
Number of battle casualties, 51,748.
Deaths from diseases, 6,767.
Other deaths, 1,003.

Decorations earned by Canadians: Victoria Cross, 62; Military Cross, 2,886; Royal Red Cross, 339; Distinguished Conduct Medal, 1,945; Military Medal, 12,041; Meritorious Service Medal,1,354; Mentioned-in-Despatches, 5,474.

Buried in France and Belgium, 37,900.
Buried in England, 3,500.
Buried in Canada, 9,000.
On the Menin Gate Memorial are the names of 7,000 Canadians missing in Belgium. Vimy Memorial shows 11,300 missing in France.
Enlistments; 64 per cent had no previous military experience; 51 per cent were born in the Dominion; 25.2 per cent of males enlisted.

Number of men drawing pensions, 75,878.
Number of individuals drawing dependants' pension, 19,308.
Total number of individuals affected by both of these, 258,756.
Oldest known pension, 88 years.
One hundred per cent pensions, 4,400; 80 per cent, 1,400; 60 per cent, 2,300; 50 per cent, 4,l00; 40 per cent, 4,200; 25 per cent,5,300; the balance of 52,700 receive below 25 per cent.

Country where pensionable disability originated:
France -   65,779 (86.7 per cent),
England -   6,768 (8.9 per cent)
Canada -   2,891 (3.8 per cent)
Other Theatres of War - 440 (0.6 per cent)

April 15th, 1933

TOWARDS THE end of the war our old platoon sergeant grew very nervous. Many new men had joined us, and one of them startled him badly by starting to walk in his sleep when we were in the dugouts down Arras way. Thereafter the sergeant watched him closely, convinced that the lad was not right in his mind. In September we were at Dainville, and billeted in a house where there was a huge clock. One of the boys, knowing the sergeant's fears, bet the new man that he could not stand in front of the clock and twist right and left as the pendulum swung, saying, in time, "This way-that way ! This way-that way!" If he could do so for five minutes he was to win ten francs, which was a sum those days.

We got him started as the sergeant was coming, and all hid. The sergeant stood a moment, staring. Alone in the kitchen was the new man, tense, excited, swaying before the clock, and repeating his ritual.

"Help-help!" roared the sergeant, and tackled him from behind with a zeal only matched by the new man's terror at being seized by a maniac.

Fourteen platoon never forgot that struggle.

When Easter is late there are new greens in the cemeteries of Flanders, and the wreaths that are placed seem more beautiful than at any other time of the year. Many pilgrimages are made from England at this date, and there is no more fitting time to have a wreath placed on the grave of a loved one.

The Hill 60 Shrub is fast becoming one of the most popular blossoms taken from the battle field. It is now being grown in thousands of English gardens, and its beauty is being recognized everywhere. It blooms in June and July, and its leaves seem to change tints continually until December. The shrub literally covers Hill 60, yet, strangely, is not noticed elsewhere in the Salient and the people there say it was unknown by them until after the war. Lawrence E. Brooks, 40 Boulevard du Nord, Ypres, Belgium, has supplied many with the seed, and will fill any order for a packet.

On Sept.12th,1916, a patrol of the 2nd Canadian Mounted Rifles at Mouquet Farm, on the Somme, found three members of the 51st Australian Battalion who had been nine days in No Man's Land. Two of them were wounded, and the unwounded comrade had chosen to remain with them. He had kept them alive by foraging food and water from the equipment of the dead that covered the battle ground. Private. S.H. Warn, of the 29th Canadian Battalion, was found at St.Eloi after he had lain in No Man's Land for nine days. He was wounded in the forearm, left thigh and scalp, and had trench feet through being so long in the chilling March mud. He was found by the 2nd Canadian Pioneers and carried to the Bedford House Dressing Station. He had lived on food taken from the dead of the British Third Division. The record case, however, is that of a private of the Inniskilling Fusiliers. He was found near Beck House Farm, at Frezenberg, by Sergeant. Finney, on the 5th of Sept., '17, after he had lain in No Man's Land for thirty-one days. He was badly wounded in both legs, yet had crawled half a mile from the spot where he had first fallen. He had subsisted on food and water from the dead in the area between the lines, and had been too utterly bewildered to attempt to reach his own trench.

I have an issue of *The Strafer*, "done into print by the 66th Battery, Canadian Field Artillery." Its first admonition is to "put your hand out and see if you are not in bed." The editor is Cpl. E.E. Carncross, the date December, 1917. Censor Major S.C. Oland. The editorial reads: "We greet you from the Front. Let's all say Merry Christmas. Of course, if you were our best girl there would be a little more after mother had left the kitchen. We are all very happy over here. We only kick for exercise, we only grouse because we imagine things, we only duck shells because we don't want them to hit us. Mud and rain and darkness are only trivial side-issues. Merry Christmas."

> Whistle, whistle, little shell,
> How we know your sound so well.
> In our hearts we`ll hold you dear
> If you whistle on by here.

It gives a stimulating account of a German prisoner :

"Several days ago, while playing left field in a baseball match in No Man's Land, a German slipped in a shell hole, and stunned himself. He was at once pounced upon by our Headquarters Staff and brought back for questioning. He spoke excellent English, and was interviewed by our *Strafer* representative.

"Referring to our recent shrapnel barrage, he said some of the shells were still on the way, some never got there at all, and some, in their excitement, went several hundred yards beyond. Shells from our rubber gun bounded for several days and had devastating effect on the superstitiously inclined. He stated that their egg-and-chip canteens in the reserve trenches were doing a Russian business, that our anti-aircraft fire was so deadly no German plane dare go more than ten miles back of our lines, that the Kaiser was swinging the lead for "Blighty," and that the S.O.S of Thursday night was caused by someone hitting the Crown Prince in the neck with a rotten apple and knocking his gates ajar collar out of plumb, that Canadian prisoners tested higher in shell grease than any of the Allied troops up front, and that the Girl Scouts of Berlin were giving a Grand Ball in their listening posts."

We searched him for souvenirs and found only a pamphlet (for officers only) on, *How to Give Hell to Gunners and Drivers*. It taught so little, due to our present efficiency, that we destroyed it, then took a rusty French bayonet, packed our prisoner in four empty shell boxes, wrapped the whole in camouflage and addressed it to the Salvage Corps for forwarding to the Maconchie Stew Co., Glencarrots, Scotland."

During the retreat from Mons many guns were abandoned after being rendered unfit for use. A total of 80 were missing. Four 4.7-inch guns of the 2nd London Heavy Battery were lost during the second battle of Ypres. 172 guns were lost in December, '17, and in the March drive 981 were lost. The grand total for the war was 1,237 guns of all calibre.

April 22nd, 1933

WHEN WE had our Christmas dinner at Souchez they called for volunteer waiters, cooks' helpers, etc. Paddy Flynn was among the first to respond and, when the hour came, had a post of honor at the C.O.'s table. There were several paunchy, red-tabbed guests, and great was the consternation when Paddy appeared with the first course - soup- his thumbs completely immersed.

"Flynn," hissed the nearest officer "take your thumbs out of the soup."

"It's all right, sorr," came Paddy's serene answer. "It's not hot at all, at all."

There was 24.02 per cent of the male population of England enlisted in the Great War, 23.71 per cent from Scotland, 21.52 per cent from Wales, and 6.14 per cent from Ireland. New Zealand led the Overseas lists with 19.35 per cent of her total white male population. Canada had 13.48 per cent, Australia 13.43 per cent, and South Africa 11.12 per cent.

Total number enlisted in Australia, 416,809. Total who served outside of Australia, 331,781. Number of battle casualties, 53,404.

Deaths from diseases, 3,919.

Other deaths, 809.

Decorations earned by Australians, Victoria Cross, 65; Distinguished Service Order, 619; Military Cross, 2,366; Royal Red Cross, 187; Distinguished Conduct Medal, 1,767; Military Medal, 9,917; Meritorious Service Medal,1,220; foreign decorations, 1,023.

Of the Australian Imperial Force who embarked 257,963 were born in Australia,

64,221 in the United Kingdom, 4,214 in New Zealand, 2,246 in other British countries, and 3,137 in foreign countries.

In 1929, 73,436 Australian veterans were drawing pensions. The oldest soldier killed in action was an Australian, Pte. H. J. Gibbs, aged 64, of the 14th Battalion, killed on the Somme in 1918. Pte. Duncan Allan, of the lst Australian Battalion, was 64 when he enlisted in June, '15. He was invalided home in '17.

Ernest Albert Corey, a stretcher-bearer in the 55th Australian Battalion, was the only man of all the millions who took part in the war to be awarded a third bar to the Military Medal. He was recommended for the D.C.M. on six separate occasions; the results were the M.M. and three bars. 481 Aussies won a bar for their M.M., and 15 got a second bar. 27 won a bar to the D.C.M. 171 won a bar to the M.C., and 4 got a second bar.

Australia has many war memorials. The most unique was at Harboard, Victoria, a dilapidated, weather-worn bungalow, once the home of five boon companions. The war came, they enlisted. Today the furniture remains as they left it when rising from their last meal. A lantana bush is growing across the front door. Overseas are five graves.

Everyone has read of the famous "Lone Pine" at Gallipoli, which gave its name to the fiercest battle between the Turks and Australians. A corporal, whose brother was killed at the foot of the tree, took a cone from the tree home as a souvenir. The cone was kept until 1928, when two seeds dropped from it, and the corporal's mother planted them in pots, and carefully tended them. Now they have grown into sturdy saplings. One is at Canberra, the Federal capital, the other in the corporal's home town, Inverell.

The following is a copy of authentic orders found in a pillbox at Passchendale, in 1917, on its re-capture. The Australian gunners who had occupied it, lay there- dead.

"1. The position will be held and the Section will remain here until relieved.

2. The enemy cannot be allowed to interfere with this position.

3. If the Section cannot remain here alive, it will remain here dead; but in any case it will remain here.

4. Should any man, through shell-shock or any cause, attempt to surrender, he will remain here--dead.

5. Should all the guns be blown up, the Section will use Mills grenades or other novelties.

6. Finally, the position will be held as stated."

A copy hangs in the Talbot House, Poperinghe.

How many brands of cigarettes were smoked in the trenches? I can remember Ruby Queens, Gold Flakes, Players, Capstans, Black Cats, Abdullas, Oro, Woodbine, 'Arf a Mo', Red Hussars, Vice Regal, B.D.V., Over Seas, Britannia, and Regents. Anyone know of more?

I have a copy of *The Daily Panic*, dated Dec. 7th, 1916. It was issued by the 2nd Artists Rifles. Its first appeal is RECRUITING. "Everybody's doing it- H.G. Wells, the Freemasons, the Oddfellows, the Spectator and others. We feel that we must do our bit and propose to send the following to all advertising their little bit in the 'Births' columns of our contemporaries.

" Open Letter to Mothers' "

"Send your babies to the Artist Rifles and be relieved of all further expense. You find the babies, we find the food and clothing. Little golden-haired, blue-eyed darlings (must be males) received and carefully cared for- mentally, morally and physically. Has your boy a special bent? We will straighten it. Does he blush? We will cure him. He over-eats at home? He cannot here. Does he swear? We can beat him.

"Note what others say of us:

"Mrs. Gooson writes: 'Very grateful for all you are doing. Can hardly recognize my boy now.'

"Mrs. Willowfry: 'We can hardly believe that Samuel is our child. We cannot understand your system.'

"Lieut. Soloot: 'My brother seemed very like a fool. Thank you for making him perfect.'

"Little Bo-Peep (Shepherd's Bush): 'I know I can trust you because my boy is in your battalion, and there is nobody quite like him.'

.. What further comment is needed? Roll up with your babies, in any shade, tenor or bass."

April 29th, 1933

REMEMBER THE white-washed corner at Queant, the spot they used as an operating room? There was a doctor in charge for a time who wore a rather long beard. One of our section was an imaginative little fellow who stammered. A shell bashed in the trench at his post and when he recovered consciousness he was in a strange white-walled place, with a white-robed, bearded person regarding him gravely.

"I s-s-s-say," piped our lad, a trifle delirious, "W-what's your name?"

"Peter," said the doctor, just to humor him.

The lad moaned- "S-s-s-saint Peter?" he queried.

Newfoundland contributed a total of 11,922 of all ranks to the fighting forces of the Empire, made up as follows:

The Royal Newfoundland Regiment	6,264
Recruited in Great Britain	62
The Newfoundland Forestry Corps	500
The Royal Naval Reserve	2,053
Enlisted in units in Canada	3,000
Nurses serving overseas	43

Their casualties were:

Killed in action	588
Accidentally killed	2
Died of wounds (including 15 in German hands)	254
Missing (presumed dead)	259
Died of sickness (including 15 in German hands)	95
Died by suicide	1
Accidentally drowned	2
Died by violence (in German hands)	1
Killed in hospital air raid	1
Deserted	10
Total	**1,213**

Honors and Awards: 1 Victoria Cross, 2 C.M.G., 4 Distinguished Service Order, 31 Military Cross, Bar (second awards) thereto 6; 31 Distinguished Conduct Medal, Bar thereto 1; 107 Military Medals., Bar thereto 8; 17 Meritorious Service Medals, Foreign decorations 23.

Arrogant Musketry Sergeant, to Tired Recruit: "And now, what would you call a fine sight?"

Tired Recruit: "A ship crammed full of sergeants, 400 miles from shore, on fire, sinking, and in a hurricane."

Old Bill tells that while on leave he got in a railway carriage with two Yorkshiremen who eyed each other steadily. Then one blurted:

"What are tha' staring at?"

"Thee, bai gum," said the other. "Tha art ugly."

"Ah knaw ah'm ugly," came the answer, "but Ah ca'ant do anythin' abaht it."

The other pondered a moment. "Oh, yes, tha can," he said sadly. "Tha can stop at hoam."

I have a copy of the *Third Battalion Magazine -Australian*, dated August, '18, and it contains some fine contributions. One of the best titled, "The Battery Horse."

"He whinnied low as I passed by,
It was a pleading sort of cry;
His rider, slain while going back,
Lay huddled on the muddy track.
And he, without a guiding hand,
Had strayed out on the boggy land;
And held there by the treacherous mire,
He lay exposed to shrapnel fire.
He was a wiry chestnut steed,
A type of good Australian breed;
His load was eighteen-pounder shells,
The sort that in a barrage tells.
I drew the shells from out their sheath
And cut his girth from underneath,
Then lifted off his saddle pack
To ease the weight and free his back.
His muzzle softly nosed my hand
Because I seemed to understand.
My steel hat from an old-time trench
I filled three times his thirst to quench;
I brought my ration biscuits back
And fed him from my haversack.
No horse that has been stable fed
More proudly tossed his chestnut head
Because a stranger saw his need,
And, passing, stayed to give him feed.
But time pressed on, I must not stay,
Four weary miles before me lay.
He made a gallant bid to rise,
Then sank with almost human sighs;
I hoped a team might see his plight,
And draw him out before the night.
Now, you may ask, why in this strife,
When times were grim and death was rife,
I should have ventured from my course
To try and help a battery horse?
I'll tell you why I felt his need ,
I've owned and loved a chestnut steed."
                    L.-Cpl. E. R,. Henry.

There were 51,308 horses killed by gunshot and 67,532 wounded. 178 were killed by gas, and 1,868 were rendered unfit by the effects of gas. The Memorial to the 58th London Division, at Chipilly, on the Somme, is most unusual. It represents (life-size) a stricken horse on a battlefield, his driver beside him holding his head. The most famous war horse was "David," of the 107th Battery, Royal Field Artillery. He served throughout the South African War, 1899-1902, and as a wheeler in a gun team went to France with the battery in August, '14, and served throughout the Great War. He qualified for the Queen's Medal with 4 clasps, the King's Medal with two clasps, the 1914 Star with bar, War, Victory and Long Service Medals, and had 4 wound stripes. The Duchess of Portland took David to her Home of Rest for Old Horses, and he died in his sleep in 1921.

Chapter 5: May 1933

May 6th, 1933

WHEN THE imaginative little fellow in our Number Three Section first joined us he was very nervous, so much so that Sergeant Jimmy Davies kept an eye on him when he went into the trenches for the first time. The second night in, old Heinie shelled us hotly for nearly an hour. When it was over the Sergeant remembered the new man and rushed to see how he had fared. He found him huddled on the fire-step with a ground sheet over his head. "Snap out of it," ordered Davies.

But there was still considerable noise and the fellow never heard him, so Davies jabbed him in the centre with his thumb as he shouted next time.

The little man's arms shot upward with great promptness. "K-k-k-kamerad!" he yelled.

Arrangements have been completed for the Belgian Government to preserve 180 of the "pillboxes" in the Ypres Salient. Up to 1931, more than 2,000 of these remained, but the Government then made a determined effort to assist the landowners in removing them. Representatives of the British Legion, Toc H, and the Ypres League called a special meeting, and their delegates asked that a number of the "pillboxes" be preserved as memorials. The Belgian Government at once suspended demolition, and asked for a list of the strongholds desired. Colonel E.G.L. Thurlow, D.S.O., prepared all information, maps, etc., and the Belgians agreed to preserve all points requested. Col. Thurlow is now preparing a guidebook which will give a brief description of the events connected with each of these strongholds. One of the most famous among them will be Cheddar Villa, at St. Julien. In Aug., '17, the "Ox & Bucks" were using it as a first-aid post when a shell exploded in the doorway killing 20 and severely wounding 12 others. Captain Hughes, the medical officer, at work, was not injured.

The songs of war time can be divided into eight categories. First, the satire on war, mock-heroics, the cold eye and literal tongue turned upon what lies back of flag-flapping and speech-making. "I Don't Want to Die," and "If the Sergeant Steals Your Rum," were samples. Then came satire on the military system, and, in order, satire on superior officers, and panegyrics of civilian bliss, the celebration of drink, as "Here's to the Good Old Beer, Drink it Down." Sixth, came nonsense, as "Inky-Pinky Parley-vous," and "I Have No Pain Dear Mother Now." Then sex ribaldry, headed by "Mademoiselle from Armenteers, and, lastly, sentimental songs, as "Rolling Home," and "The Old Barbed Wire."

Some of the most popular heard in any dugout or billet were "Apres La Guerre Finie," "At the Halt on the Left Form Platoon," Skibboo," "We're Here Because We're Here," "The Bells of Hell," "Send out the Army and the Navy," and "I've Lost My

Rifle and Bayonet." The Song of the War could be heard in the estaminets before any big push.

> *"I want to go home-I want to go home;*
> *The bullets they whistle, the cannon they roar;*
> *I don't want to go to the front any more;*
> *Take me over the sea,*
> *Where the Alleyman can't get at me.*
> *Oh, my! I'm too young to die-*
> *I want to go home."*

> *The Canadians had one of their own:*
> *"China wall, China wall,*
>   *Where the flares are low-*
> *Belgian rats as big as cats*
>   *Softly come and go.*
> *Weary, dreary China wall, where the whizz bangs fall.*
>   *If you peep you're sure to sleep by Wipers China Wall."*

And another:
> *"Keep your head down, Canadian, keep you head down, pretty boy.*
> *Last night, in the pale flare light,*
> *Fritz saw you; he saw you-*
> *You were mending your barbed wire*
> *When he opened rapid fire;*
> *If you want to see your mother, your father or your brother,*
> *Keep your head down, Canadian."*

Then there was the glorious "mowing" song, so irritable to sergeant-majors trying to still a hut at night:

"One man-two men-three men, went to mow a meadow. . . ."

Even the army expressions are gradually fading away, and perhaps it is as well that some are forgotten. But, remember when "Pip Emma, Ack Emma, Any more for any more, Archies, Toot sweet, Before you joined up, San Fairy Ann, Blighty, S.I.W., S.O.L., A.W.O.L., Brass Hat, Buck Shee, Burgoo, Fini Kaput, Zig-Zag," and a thousand other expressions were fifty per cent of the conversation?

On the march one heard : "What did you do in the big war, daddy?" Are we down-hearted? Sure we are." Meeting another battalion: "Thank God, we've got a Navy." Then, "Some say `Good old Sergeant,' but I say. . . ." In billets in bad weather: "Send her down, Davy," and "Roll on, duration." Getting ready for parade: "Ah-ah! no--- shave this morning? Ah- ah ! No-razor "

And the bugle calls: "I bought a horse, I bought a cow, I bought a donkey. . . ." Didn't it sound sweet in the dawn? "Fall in A, Fall in B," "Come to the cookhouse door, boys." Officers' mess had many rhymes, some hardly fit for publication. Then

"Letters from Lousy Lou," and "You can be a defaulter as long as you like, as long as. . . ."

Last Post was left unworded. Its beauty stilled every tongue.

The Cockneys were the best. They had a language of their own, and richly flavoured. I heard one, after a calling-down, as the officer left, say, "'E don't 'arf want 'is liver scrapin' this morning." Then came his mate's retort: "No nimes- no pack drill."

May 13th, 1933

One rainy day back at billets the boys got Paddy Flynn to referee a boxing match between Murphy, the company cook, and Doucette, a very swarthy French-Canadian from the transport section. Doucette was much the better boxer and landed a heavy right-hander. Paddy's partiality towards his countryman became very conspicuous as he began to count.

"Murphy, you fool, kape our hands up whin he rushes- ONE- and use your left to his face- TWO- ye kin bate him if you'll watch where he's hittin'- THREE- anyhow, the dirthy brute is grinnin' at ye- FOUR- remember, Murphy, ye are an Irishman- FIVE-"

It lasted nearly five minutes, and when Murphy finally got up, Doucette was so infuriated with the count that he rushed in to make a kill- and caught a wild swing flush on the chin. He had not hit the floor before Paddy was counting.

"Wan, two, three, four, five an' five is tin. Ye're out ye black baist!"

The first British officer of all the fighting services to be killed in the War- on August 6th, 1914, when *H.M.S. Amphion* struck a mine- was Staff-Paymaster Joseph T. Gedge, R.N.

One of the features of the Salisbury Plains is the clean glowing whiteness of the huge badge of the Australian Imperial Force, cut in the chalk of the hillside, which is visible in all its detail for miles distant. Sixteen years ago the Australians who were quartered in that area carved their badge, the rising sun, with the crown in the centre, and the words, *Australian Commonwealth Military Forces*, on a gigantic scale. Alongside are the badges of the 6th City of London Regiment, and of the Y.M.C.A., almost as big. A local branch of the Toc H keeps them weeded and perfectly clean.

During the war a parish priest came across Mrs. Murphy in a state of distress. "Paddy's gone," she mourned. "The poor man."

"Too bad," sympathized the kind father. "When did the telegram come?'

"Telegram!" sniffed Mrs. Murphy. "I had a word direct." And she handed the

priest a postcard covered with Pat's scrawling, which read:
"Dear Mother, I am now in the Holy Land."

There were 7,620 German officers and 311,878 other ranks taken prisoners on the Western front, together with 10,429 Austrians. A total of 463,907 prisoners were taken during the war, 6,419 being captured at sea. 43,308 civilians were interned. 1,767 Germans, 589 Austrians, 11 Turks, 8 Bulgars and 16 others were interned in Canada during the war.

On the Macedonian front 2,871 Bulgarians, 135 Germans, 27 Austrians and 144 Turks deserted. 33 officers and 416 men deserted to the British in Egypt. There escaped from Great Britain, France and Italy, a total of 6 officers, 619 other ranks, and 17 civilians. From other theatres, 10 officers, 1,235 other ranks, and 120 civilians escaped.

There were 6,482 British officers and 163,907 other ranks taken prisoners on all fronts during the war. In addition to these were 430 Indian officers, 10,864 other ranks; 236 Canadian officers, 3,493 other ranks; 173 Australian officers, 3,911 other ranks; 10 New Zealand officers, 488 other ranks; 70 South African officers, 1,468 other ranks; 6 Newfoundland officers, 144 other ranks, making a grand total of 7,407 officers and 191,652 other ranks.

Forty-seven British officers and 358 other ranks escaped from prison camps. In addition were 1 Canadian officer, 99 other ranks; 2 Australian officers, 41 other ranks; 2 New Zealand officers; 1 Newfoundland other rank; 7 South Africans other ranks; 2 naval officers and 13 other ranks - a total of 54 officers and 519 other ranks from the Western Front. The grand total in escapes on all fronts was 93 officers and 617 other ranks.

During the war the Germans offered $5,000 reward for the capture of Air Commodore Charles Rumney Sampson, the "Captain Kettle"- on account of his pointed beard- of the air forces. He made the first seaplane experiments, the first cross-country night flights, the first ascent from the deck of a warship while steaming, and had many decorations. Spies credited him with having much to do with the evolution of the Tanks, and so the reward was offered.

Capt. Albert Ball, at the time of his death, May 8th, 1917, had won more fighting honors than any Empire soldier. He was the first man to win the Distinguished Service Order and two bars. Colonel W.A. Bishop, our Canadian airman, has the Victoria Cross, D.S.O., with bar, Distinguished Flying Cross, Military Cross, Croix de Chevalier, Legion of Honor, and French Croix de Guerre with palm. In the infantry, ieutenant-Colonel H. Murray, of the Australians, has the V.C., C.M.G., D.S.O., with bar, Distinguished Conduct Medal, and French Croix de Guerre.

Since the war there has been continuous rumor that Captain Ball had not the victims to his credit that have been cited in making awards. It is said that great publicity was given his feats, and that they were deliberately exaggerated, to off-set the glamour of the famous, German Baron, the Red Knight of Germany.

In the Australian War Memorial Museum can be seen an artificial, leg, worn by a soldier who passed every medical examination, and got into the army marked "perfectly fit"-with a wooden leg. The Australian War Museum is the pride of the "Diggers" down under, and has few equals, if any.

Our Billy Guild was a dashing boy with the ladies. Badly wounded, he was being watched anxiously by a pretty nurse at the field hospital when he recovered consciousness-and kissed the face so near his own.

"Gracious!" gasped the girl. "I'm so glad you're better. That-er-kiss (she colored nicely) proves it, and it will be a feather in my cap."

"Feather?" whispered Billy.

"Yes, you're getting better-like that."

"Then," encouraged Billy, ``you just-stick around-and I'll-make you-think you're -Pocohontas."

On the 2nd of May, at the Arleux Loop, a 29th Battalion patrol captured a German runner carrying important messages to Number 6 Company of their 69th Battalion.

On the 1st of May, 1916, in the Zillebeke sector, 20 Germans tried to raid the trenches of the 49th Battalion. The "Forty-niners" saw them coming and were ready. Few of the would-be raiders returned to their lines. Nearly all were shot down. The officer and non-com. in charge were both captured. They belonged to the 121st Wurtemburgers. The Non-Comissioned Officer died of wounds.

May 20th, 1933

AT THE corner where the road in Bapaume branches toward Albert there have been several motor accidents. In '31 the debris of a car was piled there and beside it a striking inscription, painted on the end of a beer barrel:

"They gathered up the pieces
    With a dustpan and a rake
Because he grabbed a silken knee
    When he should have grabbed the brake."

The "over-the-top" king of the Great War died in 1929. He was Sergeant. Sidney Darnell, D.C.M., of the Northamptonshire Regiment. He went "over the top" on 44 separate occasions, and was wounded severely on his 45th try.

Dr. George Allan Maling, who died July, 1929, had the record of the fullest day as a medical officer. During the battle of Loos, Sept., 1915, while serving with the Royal Army Medical Corps, he worked incessantly, exposed, in the open, from 6.15 A.M. on the 25th until 8 A.M. on the 26th. During that time he personally bandaged and treated 301 badly wounded men, was continually under shell fire and in full view of the enemy lines. At 11 A.M. on the 25th he was struck down and rendered unconscious by the bursting of a large high explosive shell which did fearful havoc, leaving him without an assistant, and killing many of the men he had just bandaged. An hour later a second shell buried him and his instruments, smothering the patient he was treating, yet, when uncovered, he at once carried on with his work. He was awarded the Victoria Cross.

Who was the youngest soldier of the war? F.H. Lattimer, of North Melbourne, Australia, was born December 31, 1899. He enlisted Sept., 1914, served with a Trench Mortar Battery in France, was wounded, and was home before he had reached his 18th birthday. Pte. C.A. Mitchell, of Belmore, Sydney, was born Feb. 9, 1900, and enlisted with the 53rd Battalion, Australian Imperial Force. Was wounded July 19, 1916, and taken prisoner. Younger than either is Wilfred Hodgkinson, who was born in 1903. He served in the Navy, and lost an arm at Zeebrugge.

The Thirteenth Annual Report of the Imperial War Graves Commission contains some interesting items. 672,000 headstones have been erected over soldiers' graves in 2,500 cemeteries, and there are 86 Memorials to the Missing. The total personnel employed by the Commission is 703. In 1922 it was 2,633. There will be a further reduction this year. About 125 natives are also employed.

Last year saw the completion of the last two Memorials to the Missing in France, at Faubourg, d'Amiens, Arras, commemorating 39,925 dead, including all of the Air Services who were missing on the Western Front, and that at Thiepval, Somme, where 73,357 dead are commemorated. Other Memorials completed are at Zeebrugge, Constantinople, at Lagos Colonial Church, at Aden, at Bombay, at Shillong, in Assam, and at Noyelles-sur-Mer Chinese Cemetery in France, commemorating 46 missing of the Chinese Labor Corps. There were 47 of these, but on the removal of a hut in a Vimy area the mummified remains of a yellow man were found under the floor. The hut had been raised intact and the body pushed underneath. Those occupying the hut had complained for some time about peculiar odors, but there were many such over there in war days, and nothing was done. It was thought that the dead man had won excessively at fan-tan, as, after each pay-day; there were casualties in the Chinese Corps.

Other large Memorials are Tower Hill, London, with 12,674 names; Le Touret Memorial, with 13,480 names; Loos Memorial with 20,633 names; Pozieres, with 14,688 names; the Menin Gate, with 54,896 names; Ploegsteert, with 11,447 names; Tyne Cot, Passchendaele, with 34,957 names; Helles, in Gallipoli, with 20,752 names; Delhi, India, with 13,516 names; Villers-Bretonneux, with 18,557 Australian names; and Vimy, 11,285 Canadian names.

Six hundred and fifty-eight sites of British Cemeteries have now been purchased by the French Government and placed at free disposal of the War Graves Commission. Bodies are being found on the Somme at the rate of 800 per year, and it is proposed to enlarge Guillemont Road Cemetery sufficiently to include 2,240 more graves. It now contains 2,257 graves, including United Kingdom, Canadian, Australian, South African, Newfoundland, French and German burials.

In Belgium the sites of the 152 British Cemeteries have all been placed at the disposal of the Commission, and Bedford House Cemetery, Zillebeke, has been enlarged to contain all bodies being found in the Salient. 615 members of the Commission serve in France and Belgium, 545 being in the Horticultural Dept. 401 cases of sickness were reported during the year, 67 members being on the sick list in March, when influenza was prevalent. A Lady Medical Officer and Nursing Sister are in charge. 30 cases were taken to hospitals. The Eton Memorial School at Ypres has an attendance of 92 children; and 75 are the children of Commission employees. The Commission's School at Arras has 27 enrolled.

There were 1,221 bodies recovered from battle areas during the year. Effects were found on 963 of these bodies and 200 were identified. 34,500 bodies have been found since the war ended. There are 80,000 war graves in the United Kingdom, 2,200 in the Irish Free State, 6,500 in Canada, 4,253 in Australia, 2,672 in New Zealand, 2,433 in South Africa.

Poles who came to the War areas to assist in the clearing of the battle fields, do most of the work of recovery. These chaps are energetic at any task. I saw one husky working in a ditch near Thelus, and asked him, "Why do you work so hard?"

"To maka de money," he said. "And why so much money?" "To buy plenty beef." "And why the beef ?" "To maka me strong." "And why strong?" "To diga de ditch," he grinned.

May 27th, 1933

THE COLONEL got a new horse at the same time a young Cockney joined our Company. When the pipes started their discord on the morning parade the horse began to get excited, and the front ranks became so interested in its antics that they bunched awkwardly.

"Ease off there," shouted the captain. "Ease off."

"No, 'e ain't," yelled our Cockney in great glee "but I bet 'e will be."

One of the most interesting entries- to Canadians- in Earl Haig's despatches concerning the spring operations of 1918, is the following: "If the enemy onslaught had broken through my lines I had made arrangements whereby I was to use the Canadian Corps for counter attacks." Any student of war records can readily discern that the Canadian Corps was recognized as the "spearhead" of the British Expeditionary Force.

Do you know how many men were blinded in the war? Great Britain and her Dominions, 2,270; France, 2,500; Germany, 2,700; Italy, 1,519. Figures from the rest are not available.

Who first wore khaki? The honor is claimed by the 52nd Oxfordshire Light Infantry. Lieutenant-Colonel G. Whittal, Commanding Officer of the 52nd, contributes the following extract from the regiment's historical records, dated July 2nd, 1857, when they were marching from Sialkiot to Delhi. "This action is generally known as the combat of Trimmoo Ghat. The audacity with which the Sepoys and Sowars attacked on this occasion was not repeated in any subsequent action. Colonel Campbell had procured permission just before leaving Seaikote to clothe the regiment in Karkeerung, a native cloth of grey color, and it is supposed that this very useful and novel dress deceived the enemy as to the character of the troops opposed to them. The 52nd were the first British regiment thus clothed.
The 52nd possess historical records kept in manuscript since 1759.

A private, J.L. Williams, joined the A.I.F. with the right to place C.M.G. after his name, and caused great concern among the brass hats. He had won the honor shortly before the war, while a Secretary of the New South Wales. Justice Dept. Williams was commissioned speedily, and so the awkwardness was overcome.

The Listening Post carries the following: During our four years of the war British ships transported no less than thirteen millions of men overseas, and only lost 2,700 men through enemy action.
Five million, five hundred thousand tons of German shipping and one million of Austrian shipping were driven off the seas by Admiral Beatty's squadrons. Oversea trade and overseas colonies of the enemy were cut off, and two million Germans of fighting age were thus prevented from joining their forces. In 1916, 2,100 mines were swept up and 89 mine sweepers lost. In 1914, there were only 12 mine sweepers and patrol boats. Four years later these numbered 3,300. In order that British ships patrol

the seas they had to navigate eight million miles each month. They transported more than thirteen million men overseas, two million horses and mules, five hundred thousand vehicles, twenty-five million tons of explosives, fifty-one million tons of oil and fuel, one hundred and thirty million tons of food and other war material for use of the Allies. In one month three hundred and fifty thousand men were transported from England to France. Great Britain transported two-thirds of the American Army to France and England, and escorted one-half their total transports."

New Zealanders to the number of 128,525 enlisted for service at home and abroad. 4,314 served with British units. 98,950 served with the New Zealand Expeditionary Force overseas. 491 officers, 9,754 other ranks were killed. 198 officers and 2,760 other ranks died of wounds. 76 officers and 2,375 other ranks died of disease. 1,724 officers, 39,593 other ranks were wounded.10 officers, 488 other ranks were taken prisoners. 3 officers, 29 other ranks were missing.

The biggest German cemetery in France is at La Targette, where 39,000 German graves, black-crossed and unflowered, are attended by native laborers supervised by German officers. There are five memorials in the cemetery. These were erected by the Germans in wartime, back of their lines, and no sooner had the war ended than they were taken from their sites and placed in the cemetery. The biggest and finest one was erected in Douai, and when the impatient citizens were taking it down, to hurry it from their sight, they were thrown into a panic at the sight of a round metal container. Thoughts of a trick mine, etc., flashed through their minds, but it was discovered to be only a shell case which had been used as a container for certain records in connection with the memorial.

The Edinburgh Royal Infirmary is the largest hospital in Great Britain. It can accommodate approximately 1,000 patients. It took nine years to build.

When General Allenby was preparing for his attack on Beersheba it was necessary that a field hospital be provided for the casualties. Between sunset and sunrise three Casualty Clearing Stations were erected, with a total capacity of 3,000 beds. From a barren desert there was transformed, within thirty-six hours, an equipped hospital in which difficult surgical operations were being performed.

Paddy Flynn was bitter when he returned from his London leave. "'Tis death they are on a Catholic there," he reported. "We're not even let use thim underground cillars they have for crossin' streets."

On questioning, we found that Paddy had seen the signboard "Pedestrians" at those crossings.

War Books for the Veteran's Library

EVERY VETERAN should have the Canadian Battalion Histories on his shelf. As we have no official War History, in such sad contrast to the Australians and others, it is best to do the next best and get those unit Histories. The two recommended are the Histories of the 44th and 15th Battalions. Then there are the 13th, the 4th Canadian Mounted Rifles, the Princess Pats, the 24th, the 85th, the 14th, the 16th, and the 42nd. The latter is a very finely-bound book, as is that of the 16th, and only lacks a slight insertion at the beginning "For Officers Only." Hundreds of important incidents along the trenches at nights, patrols, listening posts-all sorts of happenings, in which the non-coms. or other ranks did some outstanding thing, are never mentioned. Veterans serving two or three years, men of the highest standard, conspicuous in every action, only have their names in the Nominal Roll.

From the Rideau to the Rhine and Back is a very fine book, the story of the 6th Field Company, Canadian Engineers. The C.M.R. have a "different" sort of battalion history, with refreshing candor, like that of the 44th, and no connection with the autocratic Records Office at Ottawa. It mentions a raid on April 27th, '18. "A picked body of raiders from `D' Company under Lieutenant F.A. Sprague, entered the German trenches, and, meeting with fierce resistance, had to kill the entire garrison. Seventeen bodies were searched, and it was found that, beyond buttons and shoulder straps, all usual identifications had been left behind. It is, therefore, most probable that these men were assembling to raid us when the assault by our men was delivered. The buttons and shoulder straps, however, proved valuable, as they showed that the lst Bavarian Division had relieved the 220 R.I.R. in front of us." That is all. No heroics on the page, though after hearing the story from one of the raiders it was easy to picture that melee. The Germans fought with the utmost courage and bravery, and it was cold steel against cold steel in a dozen cases. The C.M.R. were certainly grit to the backbone to meet the situation as they did. In May, '17, the 2nd C.M.R. had a bit of bad luck. Lieutenant Darcus was out with a working party when they put a screw stake down into a bomb of some sort, and the entire lot were wounded. The candour of the writer on page 18 is simply delightful.

Shrieks and Crashes, by W.B. Kerr, is the story of the 11th Battery, Canadian Field Artillery, and of vast interest to a former artilleryman. *Merry Hell*, by Thomas Dinesen, is a MacLean Kiltie's version of the 42nd, amusing to former members of his company, and interesting reading to those who were not. *A Blower of Bubbles*, by A.B. Baxter, *When the Gods Laughed*, by Leslie Roberts, a C.M.R., and *All Else is Folly*, by Acland, are all Canadian War Books, and of the very best.

Chapter 6: June 1933

June 3rd,1933

JOCK BURRS and Sandy McBurnie were two stout "Forty-twas,"and came from the same set of "Hielands" in bonnie Scotland, but there was considerable sourness between them. Sandy made some slighting remark about Jock's relations, and Jock drew me aside and described the very homely appearance of Sandy's wife.

"An' after they were married," explained Jock" Sandy asked the parson how much he owes him. But the parson was anither auld Scottie, an' he says `How much is it worth to you?' Sandy shookit his head and put a shillin' in the parson's hand. The parson looked at it, then at Sandy's woman, an' gie him eightpence change."

In *Medical Services*; belonging to the *Official History of the War*, Major T.J. Mitchell, D.S.O., had prepared a statistical analysis on a vast scale. The approximate total casualties in the British Expeditionary Force were 11,096,338. Eighty-two per cent of the wounded and 93 per cent of the sick or injured were returned to duty. Of the wounded who returned, 64 per cent went again to the front line. For every casualty inflicted in battle, disease claimed two, but the percentage of death from wounds and sickness was much lower than in the South African War. 86.07 per cent of the total casualties were suffered by the infantry, 7.58 by the artillery, 2.57 by the engineers, 2.46 by the machine gun corps; 1.08 by the cavalry, and 0.24 by the tank corps; 58.8 per cent were caused by shell fire, 30 per cent by bullets, 2.1 per cent by bombs, and .32 per cent by bayonet. 40 per cent of those who served at the front suffered death or disablement for which a pension is given.

There are many unique and stirring re-unions along the old battle fields. Nine German officers go each October to a point at Passchendale and there, facing the old British positions, drink three toasts to the days that were. Near Kemmel, men of a Highland Division gather every three years, and on their banquet table is a scythe. Pressed hard in those terrible days of '14, a sergeant of the Division, his rifle broken, snatched a scythe from a Belgian shed and did gory execution until the enemy was driven back.

At Fricourt, on the Somme, there gathered in 1931, one of the largest re-unions on the old fields, a grand dinner held by the survivors of the 64th Infantry Brigade. In the great attack of July lst 1916, the brigade was the only one to win its objective in that area, and held on, though many battalions could only muster 100 men. The village estaminet was draped with the Tricolor and the Union Jack. The dinner was brought from Amiens by the chef and staff of Godbert's, famous as an "Officers Only" place in wartime. Brigadier McCulloch was in the chair. The Mayor of Fricourt was a special guest, and the toast in honor of their fallen comrades was "Gentlemen, when the barrage lifts-" a toast that was first given when the officers of the 9th K.O.Y.L.I. assembled before marching up to the July lst attack. By its poignant simplicity, the toast has gained an enduring niche in English literature.

Of the total staff employed in British Government Departments 154,312 are ex-service men, a percentage of 48.97. Can any one tell me what percentage of ex-service men are employed in Canadian Government Departments?

Napoleon smoked excessively during a campaign. Wellington was a non-smoker, and issued an army order, stating :

"The Commander-in-Chief has been informed that the practice of smoking by the use of pipes, cigars, or cheroots has become prevalent among the officers of the Army, which is not only in itself a species of intoxication occasioned by the fumes of tobacco, but, undoubtedly, occasions drinking and tippling by those who acquire the habit; and he entreats the officers commanding the Regiments to prevent smoking in the mess-rooms, and to discourage the practice among officers of junior rank in their Regiments."

Seven old black horses, their average age 25, went through the war as a team, with F Battery of the Royal Horse Artillery. They went to France with the original Expeditionary Force in '14, and returned in '19 unscathed, serving in the Mons retreat, at the Marne, Aisne, Neuve Chapelle, Ypres, the Somme, and the retreat of March, '18. It was they who drew the gun-carriage at the funeral of the Unknown Warrior on Armistice Day, 1920. They are now "retired" in the country home.

Over 100,000 war widows in England have remarried, and the last census there shows that the percentage of unmarried women in the categories of those from 30 to 50 years of age is the greatest ever recorded. Great Britain and Ireland lost 623,000 single men, killed or died during war service, and so 623,000 single women lost their chance of marrying.

When we were at Mont St.Eloi rations were very slim. Paddy Flynn, after two weary evenings of inquiry, found a house at Villers au Bois where he could buy bread. The next night we met him in the village roaming about like a lost man. "What's wrong?" we asked. He explained that he could not find the house again. "An' begorra, I marked the door too," he groaned.

"Marked it?" we exclaimed. "Come along, then, we'll take a street at a time and we're bound to find it."

"But," wailed Paddy, "I marked on the *inside* so that none av th' rist could find it."

June was an exciting month with the 13th. Their history records that in '15, a patrol under Lieutenant Eagle, entered a vacant German trench and encountered a hostile party, when the officer and two of his men were wounded. In '16, they had their wonderful attack at Sanctuary Wood. On the night of the 28th June, '17, Lieutenant F.J. Smith and 8 other ranks went over to the German wire to explore. They were seen and bombed. The officer with one man as a helper, remained as a covering party while the other six were withdrawing. Major F.S. Mathewson and Sergeant W.T. Hornby went out to investigate after the main party returned, and found the man wounded, who had stayed with Smith. He reported the officer killed by a bomb, and although Sergeant Hornby took a large patrol to the spot, Smith's body was never recovered.

June 10th, 1933

OUR PADDY Flynn liked liquid of any color, and occasionally got too heavily loaded. One day at Ecoivres he was very late in joining the afternoon parade, having missed his way as he came down from Mont St. Eloi.

"You," roared Sergt. Turner. "Where have you been?"

"In-in the buryin' ground, hiccoughed Paddy.

Good old Turner was very sentimental. "Oh, sorry, Paddy," he said gently. "Who's dead now?"

"All of thim," said Paddy as he lurched into his place: "All of thim."

There have been many arguments as to which was the biggest crater of the war. The men who were at Messines contend that the Spanbroekmolen, with its diameter of 250 feet and depth of 40 feet, was the largest of them all; but the "Lochnagar," at La Boiselle, was the champion. Two very large mines were laid by the 179th Tunnelling Company, Royal Engineers, under the shoulders of the salient formed by the trenches around La Boisselle, in order to destroy any flanking arrangements, and by the height of their lips to prevent enfilade fire along No Man's Land on either side.

The southern one under the Schwaben Redoubt was called "Lochnager," and it contained 60,00 lbs. of ammonal; the other, "Y" Sap, held 40,000 lbs. The tunnel was driven from the northern flank with a gallery 1,003 feet long, the longest ever driven in solid chalk during the war. The men were barefooted, and the gallery floor was covered with sandbags. Vinegar was used to soften the chalk, and the lumps were loosened with a special bayonet, caught and laid gently on the floor. The passage was 41-1/2 by 2-1/2 feet in dimension, and an advance of 18 inches during a shift was satisfactory. In the big mine the charges of 36,000 and 24,000 lbs. were 60 feet apart and 52 feet below the surface. The mines were to be blown two minutes before zero, at 7.25 A.M., on July 1st,1916.

The Lochnager provided an enormous crater, 270 feet in diameter and 70 feet in depth, with lips 15 feet high. The German garrison of the strong point was destroyed. There were ten dugouts in the vicinity. The occupants of one, an officer and 35 men, were reached and rescued. They were in a pitiable state. The other nine dugouts were not located.

Three tunnels had been constructed across No Man's Land in the La Boiselle area. They were 8 feet in height and 3 feet 6 inches in width, and were used immediately after the assault, permitting the British to cross to the captured lines without exposing themselves to machine gun fire. The tunnels were 12 feet below the surface.

Nineteen mines were blown at Messines, using nearly 1,000,000 pounds of high explosives, and needing 8,000 yards of galleries.

Nineteen mines were used in the attack on the Somme, eight large ones and eleven small ones, yet this phase of work on the Somme is not known to the majority. Two large and nine small mines were used at Mametz, three large ones opposite Fricourt; two large and two small ones at La Boiselle; one large one at Beaumont Hamel.

The one at Beaumont Hamel was blown ten minutes before zero, and though it destroyed three sections of the garrison it served as a warning of the attack. In that sector was the famous German stronghold, "Heidenkopf." This was mined so that it could be blown up if the British occupied it. On the morning of July 1st, 1916 the German engineers lost their nerve and blew the mine too soon, destroying the garrison before the British arrived, and blocking so many dugouts nearby that the attackers were able easily to overrun all the area.

From the diary of Lieutenant Pepys:

"Up, pretty betimes, though not so soon as we intended, and there comes to me one Fusilier Lightning, whom I employ, with strong tea, cold, and biscuit, hard. Get myself ready, and so out to meet the Orderlie Sergeant.

Am greeted right civilly by the said sergeant who doth tell me it is 8.15 of the clock, that they do breakfast at 8, but that he has visited them and all is well. .

To the mess and eat my breakfast. The Senior Major doth appear somewhat melancholie, and made no answer to my salutation.

To the office. I walk with Lieutenant L'Izard who doth bespeak of a wonderful pretty maid. He tells me she hath ankles fine, and that she has consented to visit the playhouse, he to escort her. Came an orderlie with a packet, requesting that I attend the commanding officer, which I do. The colonel did take occasion to tell me about my absence from the soldiers' breakfast, which do trouble me. I discourse with him, but he of an ill-humor and severe with me.

Thence to the soldiers' dinner, where one did make complaint that his meat was raw, and yet another that his was burnt. Did cause their platters to be changed, and so satisfies. To dinner with brother officers. The colonel did bespeak me civilly, which gave me extraordinary great pleasure.

To my chamber, I having a great many military works brought me by my bookbinder, one Mr. Gale. Fell into sound sleep.

Took tea.

Did enter into an argument with an ensign as to which had greater merit, port or sherry wine. Did dress in my new red coat, from my tailor in the Pelle Melle. Very pretty, but as yet unpaid for.

To sup with my brother officers. Good viands and sweet music. After dinner, the pipes and to dancing. Very merry. The hose of the junior ensign was torn in a frolic.

Did visit the guard, and make myself acquainted with the Musketeer on sentry, who did answer with intelligence the unintelligent questions allotted to be asked and inquired into.

To my chamber, and so to bed.

June 17th, 1933

Our Sergeant Taylor was a most energetic and earnest N.C.O. "Take care of your gas masks," he ordered. "Your life depends on them, and what is more important, don't lose them or you'll have to pay for them."

His voice reminded us of verses in the Third London General Hospital Gazette :

"Now a sergeant's voice is a thing that's renowned;
It shatters the air and makes holes in the ground;
He opens his mouth, gives vent to a roar-
Down crash the houses from ceiling to floor."

He was an instructor, for a time, at Divion of the young officers of the company. One bright lad had us on parade.

"Request the men," he said, "to. . ."

"Request be 'anged," roared Taylor. ! "Give 'm boxes of chocerlates."

"When the squad wishes to form fours," said the bright lad a little later," the. . "

"As you were," bellowed Taylor. "A squad never wishes to do anythink."

He reported one member of our platoon to the C.O. when we were at Mont St.Eloi. "He's no bloody good," said Taylor. "He's lazy and he's dirty. He's never on time and he don't salute like he ought. You'd think he was an officer hisself."

At Chateau de la Haie Taylor was instructed to get the company formed up for church parade.

"Fall in," he roared. "Church of England on the right. R.C.'s on the left. Fancy religions in the rear."

We, in Canada, have the "Little Black Devils " the "White Ghurkas," the "Van Doos," the "Run, Heinie's Coming," and the "Mad Fourth," but do you know the names of some of England's most famous regiments?

The 11th Hussars are the "Cherubims;" the 13th Hussars, the "Lilywhites;" the 60th Rifles, the "Sweeps;" the Life Guards, the "Tin Bellies;" the Gloucesters, the "Back Numbers;" the Royal Berkshires, the "Biscuit Boys;" the Wiltshires ,the "Moonrakers;" the Welsh Regiment, the "Ups and Downs;" the Royal Engineers, the

"Mudlarks;" the 1st Dragoons, the "Birdcatchers;" the Royal Army Medical Corps, "Rob All My Comrades"; the Middlesex, the "Diehards;" Royal Scots, "Pontius Pilate's Bodyguard;" the Highland Light Infantry, the "Pig and Whistle Infantry."

In the army, "sergeant-major's tea" is tea with rum in it; a bayonet is a "winkle pin;" full marching order is "Christmas Tree Order;" defaulters' call is the "angel's whisper."

On Guest Night at the Mess of the 5th Battalion, Highland Regiment, one sees the Lone Drummer, who, at one time during the war, was the sole living representative of the 5th Battalion. They went into the line 450 strong. A murderous barrage was followed by a gas attack, then a huge mine simply blotted the front line out of existence. Men on the flanks could not believe that anyone survived, but heard the rat-tat-tat of a machine gun as the Germans tried to press through the gap that had been formed. Some one on the lip of the newly formed crater was using the gun with such effect that the advance was held up, and a scratch collection of reinforcements rushed up to find the drummer working the gun. He was blinded in one eye, choked with gas, with one foot gone, but was actually keeping a horde of the enemy at bay.

When he reached hospital it was found that he was covered with wounds. His powers of speech and hearing were gone, and one arm was shredded.

When you dine with the Fifth, as soon as the loyal toast has been duly honored you hear the skirl of pipes and the door is thrown open. The Pipe- major enters, followed by the Lone Drummer. Marching to the head of the table, the Drummer takes from the Commanding Officer a brimming glass of wine; with unshaking hand he raises it and gives silently the next toast-the Regiment. No words are needed.

The Judgment of Mars

(from an Australian Veterans' publication)

"A bit ago I started readin' his'try of a kind,
That people say is classical and elevates your mind.
I read of Cyprus, Pompey, and 'Annibal the Great,
Of Anthony, called Marcus, and his long-haired Gyppo mate.
I read of Alexander, the daddy of 'em all,
And good old Julius Caesar, who slipped it over Gaul.
But though these blokes were leaders, and game as Kelly, too,
They never had a war to fight the same as me and you.
The blokes that went with Caesar when he pushed along the Rhine
Didn't know the smell of cordite, nor saw a decent mine;
They knew no flamenwefer, or the stink of poison gas,
That could sweep along an earthwork and mop it up `ong mass.'
They wore a shield and breastplate and a tin 'at, all of brass,
They faced no 'Un machine gun that could mow 'em down like grass.
They never saw a `Minnie,' they never 'eard a `crump,'

They never saw a muck-up like the bombin' of a dump.
Of course, they had fatigue too, and stacks of "pad the 'oof,'
And when they struck centurions of the spit-and -polish kind
They could always get a batman from the drove of slaves behind.
And now I've summed the question up, it seems to me a joke
To boost the coves with Caesar or the Macedonian bloke;
Why, I reckon if the "Diggers" 'ad been fighting under these,
They'd 'ad to melt their statues down to give 'em all V.C.'s'

A.W. Wheen, who translated *All Quiet on the Western Front*, by Remarque, and *The Road Back*, has written a war book of his own. *The Two Masters* is the title, and it is a wonderful story of an Australian spy. Wheen is an Australian. He served with the 1st and 53rd Battalions, winning the Military Medal and two bars, and a commission.

June 25th, 1933

When Elias Greener joined us at Chateau de la Haie, he was as raw a specimen as ever was wrapped in a Black Watch Tartan. He was terribly in earnest, and so bright that he stepped on himself in trying to form fours. In the estaminet, after encouragement from the products of the Vin sisters, he unfolded his life secret- he had joined the army because he wanted a military funeral. During his first week our platoon attended a lecture in one of the huts. The subject was "Initiative and Strategy." At the conclusion the officer pointed at Elias. "What is strategy?" he demanded.

"Strategy," returned Elias eagerly, "is when you don't let the enemy know you are out of ammunition and keep on firing."

It is said that no rank of the army is derived from an English source. "Colonel" resulted from an Italian "chief of column, " corrupted by French versions. "Major" was derived from the French, and had its original derivation in the Latin word "Magnus"- meaning great. "Captain" is the oldest military title in existence and is derived from the Latin "Caput", through the Spanish "capitan." "Adjutant" comes from the French, derived from the Latin "adjutate." Sergeant" comes from the Spanish "sergento," and "corporal" from the French "Caporal." "Lance-Corporal" has a curious history. In Italy a "Lancia Spezetta" was originally a mounted trooper, who, having lost his horse, was unable to replace it, and so was turned from the cavalry into the infantry until he could re-instate himself. The Italian word implies a broken lance. "Private" is derived from the Latin word "Privatus," meaning a man deprived of rank, and hence, says Old Bill, "acting privates." "Subaltern" is the nearest to an English origin, as the "Altern" is a Saxon word meaning "elders." "Sub" is Latin.

Lieutenant-Colonel Alfred Henry Osman, who died in 1930, founded the pigeon service used in the Great War. Thousands of messages from ships at sea, from secret service agents in hiding, which might never otherwise have been delivered, were safely carried by his "flying corps." His "command" extended to every front and his birds "fought" in every theatre of war. Here are records: "Crisp, V.C." When Skipper Crisp, V.C., of the trawler "Nelson," lay mortally wounded, he scribbled a message which was carried by the pigeon of his name-and a British warship arrived in time to save the crew:

"The Salonica Grizzle" saved the lives of 250 men at Salonika when it flew through a hail of rifle fire and delivered a message which brought rescue to a stranded garrison. "Tommy's Friend" flew from a disabled tank with a message which told of massing German battalions near Amiens and enabled a British barrage to frustrate the impending attack.

"The Mine-Sweeper's Hope" carried news of the first Zeppelin attack on minesweepers, which resulted in the Zeppelin being driven off by aeroplanes.

Major R.C. Campbell, of the East Surrey Regiment, was the only British prisoner of war to be released on his own parole. He was wounded at Mons and taken prisoner. He and a party were attempting to hold a bridge at all costs, and nearly all his men were killed. Two years later, in a prison camp, word reached him that his mother was seriously ill and wished to see him before he died. He made a petition direct to the Kaiser for permission to go home, and to his great joy his request was granted. He was given a fortnight's leave, escorted to the Dutch frontier and provided with enough money to make the journey. He arrived in time to spend a few days with his mother before she died. At the end of his leave he returned to Germany. Later he was one of a party of fifteen who tunnelled their way out of a camp at Magdeburg. Major Campbell was re-captured after spending seventeen days and nights avoiding pursuers.

I JOIN UP.

(from *The Journal of the Royal Army Service Corps*)

"Jan.1. Went for a stroll and at the barracks a man with stripes on his sleeves said it was time I joined up, and I thought I might as well. He said I'd be swore at tomorrow when I see the See-Oh. They gave me tea and blankets for nothing. Not a bad place.

Jan. 2. I've promised to be a soldier for six years, and six years preserve, and if I run away I'll be run in. Got my uniform, and the tailor is going to throw a fit into them. Went to school and got `D.' I asked why, and the man said it was because there were no `E's.

Jan. 3. My foreman is a sergeant. He looked at me and said he would do his best. The others laughed and I laughed too, because I think I've made a hit. We saw an officer and the sergeant said `Shun.' I thought he said `shove,' and I gave him a good one. Now I'm going over to clean the major's coalyard.

Jan. 4. Was tired this morning and did not get up. They told me in the orderly room that everybody had to get up when the bugle blows, or C.B., but that I was abolished this time. A policeman talked to me this afternoon about my hands in my pockets, but I think I was abolished again.

Jan. 5. We had musketry practice but none of the bullets went off. The sergeant said they were 'rummies.' We had squad drill and arm drill.

Jan. 6. Am tired but can't sleep because I'm on a fatigue.

Jan. 7. Sunday, but I had to clean the gimnazeum and cut grass.

Jan. 8. I saw the Emmo and I'm going to see the See-Oh.

Jan. 16. At the rifle range. The destructor said he never saw anyone like me. I hit another man's target.

Feb. 15. I have been in detention on account of a fire in the mess. But I only used a little kerosene.

March 2. Am going to be posted tomorrow. The sergeant says I'm nearly trained now. I sat for an exam., but the fellow said the map I drew was China, and I've never seen China.

March 3. Am going on leave and don't think they want me back., but I've drawn eleven shillings so I'm going to have a splash."

Chapter 7: July 1933

July 1st, 1933

AT A certain spot on the Somme in December, '17, a road ran from the British trenches to the German lines, with only a slight barrier across it. The battalion holding the sector Christmas week sent their medical officer back with the mess cart to get all the good things necessary for a Christmas dinner. When he returned, late at night, he missed the barrier and drove into the enemy lines. Next morning they sent back the empty mess cart, with the following note:

"Thank you for all the good things you have sent us. They will be most useful. P.S.-So will the doctor, when he gets sober."

Seventeen years ago today the Battle of the Somme began. It was the first action in which all the Canadian Corps took part as a Corps. It destroyed the flower of the German Army, and almost did as much for the British. The preparations were on a gigantic scale. Orders were given for an advance of 1-1/2 miles on a 25,000-yard frontage, a drive of 4,000 yards on the right, and 2,000 yards at Thiepval. The British would sooner have attacked at any other point, but Joffre insisted on action there in order to relieve Verdun.

Plans were made for seven weeks' lodging of 400,000 men and 100,000 horses. Casualties were to be cared for by 19 main dressing stations, 39 advanced ones, and 9 posts for the walking wounded. The Royal Flying Corps had 185 planes in action, and these kept the 129 German ones opposing them from all observations. The Engineers made numerous "Russian tunnels" across No Man's Land, and laid 8 large and 11 small mines. 7,000 miles of wire cable were laid and buried and 43,000 miles of airline erected. The artillery had 1,654 guns of all calibre, giving one field gun to every 21 yards, and one heavy to every 57 yards. During the first eight days 1,732,873 rounds were fired. 800,000 trench mortar shells were provided and 35,000 smoke bombs.

The preliminary bombardments lasted seven days, but British 60-pounders and six-inch howitzers could not reach opposing enemy guns of like calibre; they were outranged. The attack was set for June 28th, but bad weather put it off two days. British airmen attacked 15 of the 23 balloons the Germans had in the air and destroyed 8 of them. On July 1st 110 pilots were in the air a total of 408 hours, and had only 8 combats. 1 German was destroyed, and 2 British.

The French would not agree to an assault before dawn, and the British troops were so heavily laden that they could not rush across No Man's Land. The attack was simply a slaughter. German gunners had ample time to come out of their concrete dugouts-which the artillery had not reached at all-and place their machine guns. Common sense and 50 seconds would have made the July 1st attack the greatest victory of the war.

A British shell penetrated Glatz Redoubt and killed an entire German Regimental Staff. In German dugouts at Ovillers copies of British orders for the attack were found posted. They had been overheard by listening apparatus. Near Beaumont Hamel a mine of 40,000 lbs. ammonal was fired ten minutes before zero and served to warn the entire line of the attack. The Newfoundland Regiment, which attacked there, lost every officer and more than 700 men. In the first day of fighting the British lost 57,470 men and officers, and captured but 25 officers and 1,958 other ranks. It was the "Blood Bath of the Somme."

The Australians lost 20,000 before they captured Pozieres Ridge. The Canadians captured Courcelette and Mouquet Farm, but lost heavily at Regina Trench. The 180th German Regiment had held Thiepval for two years and boasted that it could not be taken, but the 25th Division captured it with cold steel and desperate valor.

The total casualties for the Somme fighting were British 419,654, French 194,451, German 582,919. The German count, however, is minus their loss from the nine days' bombardment which was very heavy. The figures are not available. The British captured a total of 38,000 prisoners. They launched 98 separate gas attacks, using 1,120 tons of gas.

800 German bodies were counted in one small field at Loupart Wood. At Guillemont only 58 men of a garrison of 2,000 Germans escaped. German Regimental Histories entitle it "The Hell of the Somme," and agree that there they "lost a spirit of heroism that was never found again."

The finest of the British New Army died there, meagre yards from the German line. Pozieres is an Australian graveyard. Delville Wood, a South African one. Canadian graves are everywhere; 218 at Pozieres, 64 at Bapaume, 202 in Albert, 123 at Hebuterne, 90 at Beaumont Hamel, 563 at Regina Trench, 1,071 at Miraumont, 780 at Courcelette, 88 at Ovillers, 68 at Flers, 29 at Delville Wood; there are Canadian graves in 32 different cemeteries on the Somme. All those long slopes and gentle valleys house silent hosts, and the heart strings of three nations reach there.

Today, thank God, the guns are stilled, the dead can rest. The larks wing high again, flowers clothe the old fields and the wind is in the corn. And in Trones Wood, which was a devil's caldron of fire and steel, grave of a glorious brigade, scene of carnage beyond words to picture, there stands today a tall shaft amid the gaunt stubs and new greenery. It is a Memorial, planted there among the remnants of old machine gun posts and saps and trenches, rubble and bones, and the inscription it bears is: "This is My Command, that ye love one another."

Over in a German cemetery, in English, on a black cross, there is written: "Blessed are the peacemakers."

It is said that more than 1,160 French peasants lost their lives as they returned and began to reclaim the farmlands that were theirs before the war. Each time a spade is driven or a plough set in the furrow the grizzled farmer takes his life in his hands. It will be long years yet before the war ceases taking its toll along the valleys of the Somme and Ancre.

IN 1918, while we were at Bramshott Camp, headed homeward, it was learned that the family of Jimmy John, long our orderly corporal, who was killed at Mons, was in very reduced circumstances. Jimmy John had always been ready to help anyone, lending francs that were never returned, and so some of the leading spirits in the platoon decided to do something for his wife and children. It was thought that a raffle, with tickets at a steep price, would be more successful than straight subscriptions. Sergt. Taylor was one of the first approached by the sellers.

"A ticket on a raffle for Jimmy's woman!" he exclaimed disdainfully. "Who wants a widder?"

The first officer to have a batman was George Washington.

The first memorial of the Great War erected in Canada is at Nappan Station, Nova Scotia.

"In them civil wars," said our Old Bill, "they couldn't 'ave 'ad no sar'gint majors,"

Scene: A sun-baked sap on the Mericourt front in '17.

Characters: Old Bill and Jimmy Hughes seated on a row of sandbags, which were to be dumped back of the trench after dark.

Jimmy, wiping his brow: "I feel like a pint of beer right now."

Old Bill, his lips cracking: "Lumme, I wish you were, Jim."

In Lievin the cooks had a domain wherein arrangements were slightly cramped. Paddy Flynn was assistant at the time, and in carrying water always blundered in at the front entrance, when he should have entered at the rear. After reprimanding him several times, Bob Bittle, head cook, thrust a piece of chalk in Paddy's hands and told him to go and mark the entrances so he would know which one to enter. A little later Bob went out and inspected. Both doors bore a large and scrawling "B."

"See here, Paddy," he called. "What does this mean?"

"Oh, that one," said Paddy reassuringly, "is for `behind,' and the other one is `before' the dixies."

The King's bodyguard of the Yeomen of the Guard is the oldest Royal Bodyguard in existence, and is also the oldest military corps existing in any country. Though it can be traced back to guards of the Saxon and Norman Sovereigns, its real historical origin is to be found in the bodyguards of the Plantagenet Kings of 800 years ago. Henry VII made his Royal Bodyguard a permanent institution in 1845, and when Charles II reorganized the Royal Household he fixed the establishment of the King's Bodyguard as it is today. It consists of 4 officers, 4 corporals, 8 sergeant-majors and 92 yeomen.

War souvenirs are now being constantly returned to their original owners, or to families of the losers. Even the Australian Government has returned the name-plate of the cruiser "Emden" to Germany. Colonel G.C. Cook, an American officer, has collected from ex-doughboys more than 500 "souvenirs" and has returned as many as possible to their German owners. A German has returned the drum of the Argyll and Sutherland Highlanders, lost at Roye. Another German has returned a book of poems to the family of a Scottish soldier. He took the book in 1917 from the body of the Highlander. Three different cases are known of books of poetry being returned to German hands. An Australian has had a watch returned that was taken from his brother at Passchendaele. General Crozier, in his book, *A Brass Hat in No Man's Land*, tells of how his H.Q. had to forsake many valued possessions when leaving Lys in April, 1918. In 1924, he was dining at Cologne with a German family when he saw a silver cup, which he had donated for brigade sports, staring at him from the centre table. Photographs, books, rings, medals, watches, and many trinkets, have been returned to both England and Germany by those who seized them during the heat of battle and did not realize just what they were doing.

Montauban, on the Somme, had 274 houses; Longueval, 138; Mametz, 120; Thiepval, 93; Fricourt, 176; Contalmaison, 72; Beaumont Hamel, 162. Albert had 1,105 houses, with 6,742 inhabitants.

From 6 A.M. July lst, on the Somme, to 6 A.M. July 2nd, field ambulances collected 26,675 wounded from the battle ground. At Montauban a German dugout was found full of dead. They had been killed during the seven days of bombardment and there had been no opportunity to bury them. When the Scots Fusiliers entered the village the only live occupant was a fox. A Bavarian machine gunner was found chained to his gun.

Seventeen years ago yesterday the British 17th Division, under General Pilcher, attacked Contalmaison. The enemy, aware of the intentions, had sent a hurry call to Valenciennes for reinforcements. A strong battalion of the Prussian Guards was sent at once, but no guides met them and they had no maps or references. They advanced blindly, walking into a barrage which covered the advance of the British, and were simply annihilated. The Welsh attacked Mametz Wood at the same time, but back at G.H.Q. matters were bungled frightfully. Battalion commanders received conflicting orders, and there was no coordination, nor did the commanding officers know the tactics of the battle in which they were employed. For two days the Wood and the village ruins ran with red blood, and then the British had bayoneted the last defender in Contalmaison, capturing all that remained of the 122nd Bavarian Regiment.

When Field-Marshal Sir George Milne was General Officer Commanding the Allied Armies in Macedonia in '17, all ranks had orders to salute on sight his imposing staff car which carried a large Union Jack. One day it approached a camp where an Army Service Corps private was whiling away an hour, and the fellow was so astounded that he lost all power of action. Sir George stepped from the car.

"Haven't you been given orders what to do when you see that flag?" he demanded.

"Y-y-yes, sir," stammered the man.

"What were you told to do?" roared Sir George.

"P-p-please, sir," explained the private, "the s-sergeant told me to hop it like hell."

July 15th, 1933

DURING THE March retreat in '18 an officer of the Engineers instructed a green corporal to go and put a railway station out of commission."Make sure the Germans won't be able to use it " he finished very impressively.

At night the corporal and his men caught up with the company. Each man carried a heavy sack and seemed utterly exhausted.

"Well," said the officer. "Did you put the station out of use?"

"You bet we did, sir," said the green corporal, pointing to the sacks. "We've got all the tickets here."

When we were newly arrived in France, Sergeant Taylor and Jimmy found an estaminet near Division where they sold a sweet green mixture that had no sharp kick but quite marvellous effects. After a few drinks Jimmy straightened his belt and grew very solemn. "I'm goin'," he announced thickly, "back to see Haig. I'm goin' to join him."

Taylor also had adjusted his belt and was sitting very stiff and soldierly. "You can't see him," he announced scornfully and with a majestic gesture. "I've sent him 'ome."

Mr. C.P. Churchyard, a schoolmaster of Kent, met, last September, a German schoolmaster from Mainz-on-the-Rhine who had been on an opposite post at Boesinghe, on the Ypres Canal, in 1916. Each had been on sentry go at the same hours, had shot at the other, thrown bombs at the other, for a space of six days. So complete were the details they remembered that each was amazed, and they travelled together to the historic spot and there drank to each other's long life and prosperity.

Major Graffety, to Paddy Flynn: "Did you shave this morning?"
Flynn : "Yis, sir-yis, sir."
The Major, sternly: " Well, next time stand nearer to your razor."

The following died as prisoners of war:
Regular Army and Territorial Force - 172 officers and 6,249 men
Australian - 16 officers and 238 men
Canadian - 25 officers and 275 men
New Zealand - 2 officers and 27 men
Newfoundland - 0 officers and 31 men
South Africa - 0 officers and 61 men
Royal Naval Division 3 " 105 "
Indian Native - 1 officer and 267 men
Total: - 219 officers and 7,253 men.

Six G.C.B.s were given to France, 1 to Russia 2 to Italy, 1 to Belgium, 1 to United States. 18 G.C.M.G.s were given to France, 11 to Russia, 9 to Italy, 1 to Belgium, 4 to Japan, 2 to Serbia, 2 to United States. 34 K.C.B.s were given to France, 13 to Russia, 24 to Italy, 10 to Belgium, 2 to Serbia, 2 to Roumania, 1 each to China, Greece and Portugal, and 5 to United States. 61 K.C.M.G.s were given to France, 27 to Russia, 35 to Italy, 17 to Belgium, 6 each to Japan and Serbia, 2 to Roumania, 4 to Portugal, 3 to Greece, 1 to Siam, 18 to United States. 736 C.M.G.s were handed out to allied nations, 465 C.B.s; 1,491 D.S.O.s; 3,609 M.C.s; 9 bars to M.C.s; 4,957 D.C.M.s; 1 bar to D.C.M.; 7,389 M.M.s; 6 bars to M.M.s; 668 M.S.M.s; 327 R.R.C.s; 3 K.B.E.s; 47 C.B.E.'s; 122 O.B.E.s; 200 M.B.E.'s; 609 B.E.O. Medals.
A total of 20,974 decorations were conferred.

Seventeen years ago yesterday came the second general attack on the Somme. Contalmaison was taken on the 9th, and Ovillers became the shambles of the line. The Germans had tunnelled and burrowed until their defences were like a fortress, and there it became a matter of hand-to-hand fighting, with bomb and bayonet and clubbed rifles until, after 17 days, all that remained of the 3rd Prussian Guard-140 men-surrendered. The attack on July 14th was an assault on Bazentin le Grand and Bazentin le Petit to Longueval on the right, and Delville Wood. The Dragoon Guards with masses of Indian Cavalry were drawn up just back of the front, all the night, waiting their opening and a chance to ride into the blue. "This," wrote Sir Philip Gibbs, after the war, "was significant of the mentality of our High Command. It proved the strange, unreasoning optimism which still lingered in the breasts of old-fashioned generals, in spite of what had happened on the 1st of July, and their study of trench maps, and their knowledge of German machine guns."

A troop or two made their way over cratered ground and skirted Delville Wood; machine guns killed their horses and the riders lay all night in shell holes while German shells searched for them. The Dragoon Guards charged a machine gun in a corn field and killed the gunners, but that was all they did before pitiless machine gun fire had checked them. Then the cavalry were dismounted and put to digging trenches.

Up at Longueval, British guns shelled their own lines and killed the Scots who had gained a footing in the enemy's ground, and there was more and more of it in the three days that followed, especially at High Wood, where the Londoners were cut up badly by British heavies, all through a tangling of orders and information at headquarters. Longueval was not captured until the 19th.

A night advance on the 14th netted 1,000 yards across Caterpillar Valley, and at dawn all the German line between Longueval and Bazentin le Petit Wood was captured. Trones Wood was captured. On the 15th, Delville Wood witnessed a most desperate battle. The South African Brigade attacked -121 officers and 3,032 other ranks- won the Wood, and lost it, after five days' bitter fighting and the loss of 92 officers and 2,281 other ranks.

In France there were on November 27th, 1916 in hospitals and on ambulance trains 54,550 patients, and 614 in transit.

In France on November 22nd, 1917 there were in hospitals and on ambulance trains 100,322 patients, and in transit 1,905 patients.

In France on November 22nd, 1918, there were in hospitals and on ambulance trains 107,472 patients, and in transit 1,905 patients.

In 1917 there were among the patients 2,490 German soldiers. In 1918 there were 6,378 prisoners of war included.

CASUALTIES OF WAR

	Killed or Died of Wounds	Wounded	Missing
France	1,385,300	3,690,000	446,300
Belgium	13,716	44,686	34,659
Italy	460,000	947,000	530,000
Portugal	7,222	13,751	12,315
Serbia	45,000	133,148	152,958
Greece	5,000	21,000	1,000
Russia	1,700,000	4,950,000	2,500,000
United States*	48,909	205,690	4,526

*(Died of disease, 28,209). (United States official figures, given April 1, 1920, read): Killed in action, 35,560; died of wounds, 14,720; died of disease, 57,460; died other causes, 7,920; wounded, 205,690; missing, 46; prisoners, 4,480.).

The total permanent loss reported by the Roumanian Embassy, 6th January, 1919, is as follows: Killed and missing, 9,589 officers, 326,117 other ranks. In addition, 265,000 civilians were reported killed or missing.

Bulgaria, 77,250 killed or died, 152,390 wounded, 25,652 missing.

Turkey, 85,000 killed or died, 400,000 wounded; died of disease, 204,000; unaccounted for, including prisoners, deserters and missing, 1,565,000.

Austria-Hungary, 1,200,000 killed or died, 3,620,000 wounded, 2,200,000 missing.

Germany: (Correct figures will never be known, as after the Armistice a large proportion of their hospital registers were lost, and there are no figures available of their "died of wounds" or "died of disease," which must have been a large number. The quoted figures are from those published by a Majority Socialist Organ, Berlin, Jan. 6th, 1920.).

	Officers	**Other ranks**	**Total**
Killed -	62,693	1,655,553	1,718,246
Wounded -	116,015	4,118,092	4,234,107
Prisoners and			
Missing -	23,104	1,050,515	1,073,619
Total	**201,812**	**6,824,160**	**7,025,972**

Their Navy losses were said to be 78,342, including 24,112 killed.

July 22nd, 1933

PADDY FLYNN was a trench sentry near a low-walled stretch at Lens. One had to keep low as they travelled there, and a party from brigade were to pass that way. "Flynn," said Sergeant Taylor, "you make sure you warn the staff party about that low spot ahead. You're for it if you forget."

The red tabs were late in coming and Paddy was gone for his rations when they happened along. A regular fusillade of snipers' bullets greeted them and a major was badly winged, while another had his neck grazed. Our O.C., raging, sent for Paddy. "Why didn't you stay and warn them?" he roared.

"Sure, now," explained Paddy, pointing, "There's all that's needed, if they'd used their eyes and judgment:"

Fixed high on a stick in the parapet, at the low place, waved Paddy's bright red handkerchief, attracting every Heinie eye over the way.

The Germans had wonderful listening sets and it is amazing to scan their records and see how much they learned by such methods. Up at Kemmel, in Feb. 1915, they heard all the details of a raid by the Connaught Rangers, and were fully prepared. Zero hour was at 7.15, and they shouted, "Come on Rangers. We're ready and waiting."

The raiders were cut to shreds, only a few wounded surviving. A white flag was raised and the Germans permitted a party to recover the wounded. After the armistice, however, one of the Connaught officers was missing. He had been neatly sandbagged and gathered in as he moved too near the enemy trench.

At Vimy, in 1916, the Germans heard all the conversation between the town Major of Villers au Bois and the commanders of units in the line; they knew the number of men in billets and in the trenches, and when reliefs were made, had this information for a period of several weeks, yet, as far as can be ascertained, never made use of it. At St.Eloi the Germans heard a discussion of the March attack of 1916, and blowing of mines. They sent for experts who listened underground and said that no mines had been prepared, so the overheard discussion was believed to have been a ruse. At the Somme they overheard conversations at two different points of the line. All of this makes me think of a most amazing happening down at Parvillers in 1918. We had just captured a network of old Somme trenches that were honeycombed with undergrounds. Sam Sykes, who was killed later, entered a concrete dugout and I followed him in. We were surprised to see a candle burning, maps and papers and a telephone -one of those queer flat ones-on the table. Sam picked it up, and a perfect torrent of gutturals poured into our ears.

"Get off the line," said Sam. "You`re over time."

The voices stilled as if by magic, and there was a long, significant silence, then one mild voice inquired, in very fair English, "Who is it?"

"Lord Kitchener," said Sam, "and Lloyd George is with me. Who are you?"

Another pause, then the voice again, extravagantly polite, "Your humble servant, Von Hindenburg." And they said a German had no sense of humor.

There have been many arguments about the proportion of officer casualties to those of "other ranks." The following table is the answer.

	Officer	Men
Cavalry	1	9.4
Royal Artillery	1	12.3
Royal Engineers	1	16.4
Infantry	1	23.9
Machine Gun Corps	1	14.8
Other Arms	1	12.3
Overall Ratio	**1**	**21.0**

The proportion was, for all forces except the Royal Air Forces, 1 to 21.4.

From the *London Evening* News: FRITZ TRANSFERS.

"I had come off the guns and was on my way to billets at Maroc. Near the village a man stepped from behind broken masonry. "Hello, Gunner," I said.

"Pardon, Herr Officer." I caught my breath. "Can you please tell me ver is mein regiment?" It was a Fritz, and a very small one. .

"What the devil are you doing here?" I blurted.

"Please, I haf mein regiment lost."

"The Prussian Guards?" I asked.

"Nein," said the Kaiser's last hope. "Dis morgen I vos der Saxon Regiment, but ve fight, so I dransfer to der Nordumberlant Vussiliers, yah."

Then it dawned on me. "Oh, you've been taken prisoner?"

"Yah, Herr Officer, I dransfer meinself a brisoner. Ver is mein regiment, dank you. I loose him."

Up came a private of the Fusiliers. "Well, I'll go to 'ell," he burst forth. "Wot do yer mean by goin' an' gettin' yerself lorst. Blinkin' fine time I've 'ad chasin' yer." Then to me: "Fanks, for 'avin 'im."

"Oh, I just found him," I said.

"'Ave a pull of this." Yes, it was rum, a water-bottle full.

"Good luck to the Fusiliers," said I.

"Luck to the Gunners," he said in his turn; and then: "'Ere, Fritz, you can 'ave a swig."

The German's eyes lighted. "Prosit," he cried to mein regiment, der Nordumberlant Vussiliers:"

And then they trotted off down the road, the Cockney happy in having his lost lamb back, the Fritz happy because he had "found" his regiment; and I was happy because I had had a most welcome.and unexpected drink."

M. Laibe, the first Frenchman to be wounded in the War, died in 1932. He was a Customs officer on duty at Suacre on the frontier, Sunday, Aug. 2nd, and war had not been declared. A Uhlan detachment rode over into French territory and seized horses, carts, cattle, and several inhabitants, firing on the Customs patrol, and wounding Laibe.

July 29th, 1933

THE PRIZE boner of the War, on the British side, was pulled by the Home Dept. A high-placed red tab in Egypt needed sandbags in a hurry and cabled for them. Within a few days there arrived at Alexandria a ship loaded with the wanted bags- *already filled with sand !*

Old Bill, while in Blighty, had some tattooing done. He had a neat little boat inscribed on his "lower chest." Recently I saw Mrs. Bill and inquired about Bill's health. "His 'ealth," she snorted. "Well, you remember that little boat 'e 'ad on 'im?" I said I did. "It's a blinkin' warship now," she finished.

And old Jock Gray of our "D" Company is not getting away with all his stunts as he did in war days. Driving in the city in his old car he collided with an enemy from the region round about Jerusalem. Cohen recovered first and produced a flask as he hurried to Jock's rescue. But it took one drink, two drinks, three drinks, even a fourth, to get Jock revived-just as the traffic cop came up. "Now, then," roared the official of the roads . "Who's to blame for this?" "Vell," said Cohen mildly, pointing to Jock, "smell his breath."

In October of last year there was formally opened at Neuville-St.Vaast, near Vimy, the "Cite des mutiles et du Flambeau." At the entrance of the "Cite" stands a memorial representing the giant hand of the War Dead reaching up from the ground and grasping the Torch of Civilization, which is being passed on to the living. The "Cite" comprises about 15 houses which have been built through the efforts of French ex-service men, in order to house the "Grand Blesses" of the district, who will look after the military graves in the neighbourhood. To each house has been given the name of a well-known French General, and the only one that bears any other than the name of a French leader is the "Villa Byng," named in honor of Gen. Byng, to commemorate the grand victory of the Canadian Corps in April, 1917.

TALE OF AN OLD SOLDIER

(From Royal Army Medical Corps; *News and Gazette*).

"I got the Military Medal for capturing twenty Jerries, including a quarter-bloke, which shows 'ow quick our advance was, and what I thought was a machine gun, but a bloke from the intelligent branch wiv a lot of red on 'is 'at an' collar, said as 'ow it were a new patent German sausage machine. Anyhow I got the M.M.; and there was that bloke of the Army Service Corps at the Base, all the blinkin' war, who got the Distinguished Conduct Medal for baking rooty. I very nearly got another gong once, not quite. We was in a little one-eyed village called Omelette, or like that. They called it rest because we slept in a barn wiv the roof off instead of a dugout wiv the roof on. But I pinched twenty green envelopes and used to flog 'em one by one to my bed chum 'oo was a teetotaller for 'is tot of rum. 'E was squarepushin' some gal in Peckam and used to write 'er every day.

Well, there was a canal outside the village and me and a skinny cove called Spud Murphy went to 'ave a bath. Poor old Spud couldn't swim and it were a deep 'ole, so I jumps in and brings 'im out. Lucky there was an estaminet near, and a bit o' fluff I knew give me a bottle of Cognac, and after I'd drunk 'arf of it Spud came around. Next day 'e said 'e wanted me to go wiv 'im to see the old man, so up we goes and the Regimental Sergeant-Major marches us in.

R.S.M.: "Ptes. Murphy and Spratt to see you, sir."

C.O.: "Well, what is it, Murphy?"

Spud: "I wish to recommend Private Spratt for the Royal Humane Society Medal. 'E saved my life when I fell in the canal yesterday, and were goin' down for the third and last time."

C.O.: "Were you both bathing in the canal?"

Spud: "Yes, sir."

C.O.: "Sergeant-Major: "Isn't the canal out of bounds?"

R.S.M.: "Yes, sir."

C.O.:" Right. March them out; and march them in again, under escort."

The result was that me and old Spud got three days' number two, and I never got no medal. Old Spud got a punch on top of 'is nose, but I 'adn't the 'eart to 'urt 'im. I met Spud last week. 'E's a staff-sergeant now in the Medicals, but, oh 'ell, if 'e fell in the canal today 'e'd float."

Remember the old "tin hat." This is an extract from War Records. "A helmet made of four separate parts and weighing 22 ounces was issued to the French troops in the spring of 1915. This was brought to the notice of G.H.Q., who asked for samples for trial, and 495 were received on 29th July, 1915. The British authorities decided the protection afforded was insufficient, and after experiments a sample steel helmet was sent to France in September. A scale of 50 per battalion was furnished, and by the end of October 2,500 had been supplied. After further experiments a helmet of hardened manganese steel weighing two lbs. was adopted. It was capable of resisting shrapnel at 750 feet per second. Their manufacture was commenced in November, and by

March, '16 140,000 had been issued in France. Delivery of the first million was completed by July. One and a half million were supplied to the American troops. In Sept., 1917, issue was made to the troops at home, and by the end of the war seven and a quarter million helmets had been issued.

The German helmet was the suggestion of a German professor who served as a captain in 1915, and by the end of January, 1916, 30,000 were being worn by the shock troops at Verdun. Its weight was 2 lbs. 3 oz.

A census of traffic at Fricourt cemetery between 9.15 A.M. July 21st and 9A.M. July 22nd, 1916.

Troops - 26,536	Guns - 63
Gun carriages - 13	Motor cars - 568
Busses - 95	6-horse wagons - 1,458
Motor lorries - 813	2-horse wagons - 1,215
4-horse wagons - 568	Horses, riding - 5,404
1-horse carts - 515	Cycles - 1,043
Ambulances - 350	Machine guns - 10
Caterpillars - 10	

And from 10 P.M. to 4 A.M. the traffic Control had to wear goggles on account of tear gas, and missed counting an infantry column.

Chapter 8: August 1933

August 5th, 1933

OUR CRUSTY sergeant-major, Sandy MacBurn, scorned all who lived south of Inverness, especially those from old Scotland's busiest city. A new lad, hailing from there, joined us at Villers au Bois, and we gathered near to hear results. After the usual questions Sandy asked: "Where were ye born?"

"Glasca," said the boy proudly.

"Glasca!" roared MacBurn. "Glasca! Whatever for ?"

The newcomer, crushed by MacBurn's gaze, sought desperately for an adequate answer.

"I-I wanted to be near me mither," he pleaded.

Two members of the First Expeditionary Force sent to France were placed in charge of the rifles at Le Havre. Their battalion was rushed off to Ypres on a moment's notice and they were forgotten in the hurry. There they remained, running a small canteen, on the proceeds of which they lived. No officer ever questioned them, and they made no attempt to draw pay. When the war was over they presented themselves for demobilization, exhibiting the orders they had received and which had not been cancelled. So they could not be tried for desertion, and had to be presented with four years' back pay, their gratuity, and a clean sheet with their discharge paper . What a war it was for them!

The year 1918 was the only one during which German casualties exceeded those of the British--according to the figures that are available. British figures are correct, but the German ones have no account of those who "Died of wounds," surely a very large number, or of those who "died of disease." This must be remembered when reading any published comparisons. The figures show that there were five British officer casualties to every two German officer casualties, and that the proportion of "other ranks" casualties was about three British to two German-excepting 1918.

The Germans surrendered to the British 1,781 aeroplanes in good condition, and 942 aeroplanes in bad condition.

In 1914 the Royal Army Service Corps consisted of 498 officers and 5,933 other ranks. In 1918 it had grown to 10,477 officers and 314,693 other ranks. The casualties for the war were:

	Officers	Other Ranks
Killed in action	79	1,507
Died of wounds	42	967
Died, disease, etc.	159	5,713
Wounded	384	7,262
Prisoners of war	22	98
Total	**686**	**15,547**

In 1914 there were just 117 Chaplains in uniform. 89 were Church of England, 11 Presbyterians, and 17 Roman Catholic.

On November 11th, 1918, the following were it service:

	Home	France	Egypt	Italy	Elsewhere
Church of England	709	878	134	58	206
Presbyterian	75	161	19	8	39
Roman Catholic	78	389	54	32	98
United Board	60	126	19	12	33
Wesleyan	60	127	20	12	37
Welsh-Calvinist	4	5	1	-	-
Salvation Army	-	4	1	-	-
Jewish	-	8	3	-	-
Total	**989**	**1,698**	**251**	**122**	**415**

The first wrist watch is believed to have been worn by Captain King, of the 14th Hussars, in April, 1887. He had his saddler improvise a strap arrangement by which he could wear his pocket watch on his wrist. Officers of the 13th Hussars, however, claim to have originated the idea.

Last month saw the third anniversary of the new Cathedral of St. Martin's at Ypres. The first stone of the new building was laid on Nov. 11th, 1922, so that it took eight years to build, and the cost was more than fifty million francs- roughly, one million three hundred and eighty-five thousand dollars. It was reconstructed in the Thirteenth Century style. The first German shells struck the original building on Nov. 22nd, 1914.

An Army "crime" consists of one unpolished button on a church parade, or a boot laced wrongly. It is an exceptional soldier who is not crimed in the course of seven years' of serving. Yet there is an ex-sergeant-major, one Isaac Topps, who served 28 years with the 3rd Grenadier Guards-a most meticulous regiment-and had not a single crime marked against him. He has been awarded the Meritorious Service Medal.

More than 9,000 soldiers, sailors and airmen were treated for facial injuries at Queen's Hospital at Sidcup, where such work was handled. Many of the patients were disfigured almost beyond recognition, yet had their features restored so that but little trace of their wounds remained. Many of these men had to remain under treatment from two to four years, and several underwent as many as twenty operations. 11,752 major operations were performed, and there were many times that number of minor cases.

Sergeant Taylor organized a "sweep" while we were enjoying a "rest" at Lozinghem, and the evening of the draw Paddy Flynn came to the billet to learn results.

"Sure," said. Taylor, "it's over. I won first prize, and my buddy got second prize, and the orderly corporal got third. Ain't we lucky? But look here, Flynn. You didn't pay me for your ticket."

"No," said Flynn, "and ain't I lucky?"

The History of the 14th Battalion, Australian Imperial Force, is one of the finest unit histories yet published. The battalion boasted the:-

First Australian to win the Victoria Cross.
First chaplain killed in action.
First Anzac buried in Great Britain.
First subaltern to win the Distinguished Service Order.
Oldest soldier killed in action.
The youngest sergeant and youngest captain.
Twins killed on the same day.

On the 11th November, 1918, when shipping ceased, the Canadian Commission had shipped from North America 428,608 horses and 275,097 mules. Purchases in the United Kingdom reached a total of 468,323. South America supplied 6,000 horses and 1,500 mules. 3,700 mules were obtained from Portugal and Spain.

August 12th, 1933

"PATSY JONES, cook's helper, complained that something was wrong with his interior, and went on sick parade. After a critical examination he was given some delightful pellets known to the boys as "Number Nines," and marked "M. & D." Patsy made severe and bitter remarks as he returned to the cook wagon.

"Stow that," ordered Sergt. Taylor. "Y'er bloomin' lucky, that's wot you are. If you'd been in civil life that there consolation with a doctor would have cost you ten bucks."

Wooden crosses from the graves of "Unknown Soldiers" were presented in hundreds to Branches of the Toc H organization when stone replaced the wooden markers.

The Memorials at Vis-en-Artois, Loos, Pozieres, and Louveral (Cambrai) were all unveiled on an August 4th. This anniversary has been used more than any other date in the unveiling of memorials.

An Old Story in a New Guise

(from the The Hampshire Regimental Journal)

Secret.

ISRAEL DIVISION
Operation Order No.1

Copy No.1.

Reference:-Map SHOCHOH 1 in. to 1 mi.

Date B.C

Information.
Regarding enemy:-

At 2,000 hours yesterday it was learned that a force of Philistines, strength about 2 Div., was concentrated in SHOCHOH (A3,466) and AZEKAH (B4,567).

An itinerant purveyor of manna reports that the enemy are badly equipped, ill-fed, in arrears with pay, and that their morale is, accordingly, very low.
Regarding our own forces:-

Our troops, composed mostly of compulsory transfers from the Non-Combatant Corps, are obviously unfitted to take the offensive. There are no troops on our right or left, but unfortunately there are some in front, i.e." the Philistines.
Boundaries :

There are none, to our mutual regret.
Intention :

In view of the sorry state of the opposina forces, it is evident that an attack by either as a whole is out of the question. Personnel engaged on both sides, however, are all serving on duration-of-war-engagements, and are anxious to be either demo-

bilized or released for agricultural work. It is there fore desired to terminate hostilities as soon as possible.

A conference between our and the enemy's General Staffs was accordingly held in the valley of ELAH (D6,798) at 0600 hours today, when it was decided that a representative from each side should fight a decisive action.

Method :

It is learned on reliable authority that the enemy are sending C.S.M. Goliath, Goldstein Guards. He is armed with sword, lance, bayonet (Patt. '88) and equipped with fencing jacket, mask and steel helmet.

The Div. Commander has selected as our representative L.-Cpl. David, Israel Div. Labour Company. He will be armed ostensibly with 14 tins of plum-and-apple jam, carried en-banderol. His equipment will consist of haversack and water-bottle (filled). Secreted in the haversack however, will be one dozen Wills' hand-grenades. No other haversack ration will, or need, be carried.

Zero is 12 hours today.

At zero plus 15 minutes the Div. will be formed up in the line on ridge one mile east of ELAH (C1,234). Bands will be massed in front of centre of Div. No exemptions.

At Zero plus 20 minutes L.-Cpl. David will advance in quick time towards enemy's lines. The Bands will blow mightily (particularly performers on the Sackbut and Timbrel) in order to smother jeers of the unwashed Philistines.

When within 50 yds. of Goliath, David will halt, quickly plunge his hand into his haversack and hand him (Goliath) the merry pineapple, good and plenty.

ADMINISTRATIVE ARRANGEMENTS:
   None worth mentioning.
ACKNOWLEDGE.

Captain of the Host
for Col. G.S., Israel Div.

Issued by our chariot-driver at 0,800 hours to:-
   Our side.

SPECIAL ORDERS OF THE DAY
By Saul, Commanding Israel Division.

Date B.C.

Part Two.

The C.O.C. has great pleasure in placing on record the successful conclusion of today's operations. The enemy have a vacancy for a C.S.M. and have retired in the direction of GATH (Y6,789).

In consideration of his exceptional services, L.-Cpl. David is promoted to Temp. Lieut. as from this date. Further, he is appointed A.D.C. to the Div. Com. and granted the rank of A-Capt., with pay and allowances of a Staff Lieut. (Class G.G.) whilst so employed.

The head of C.S.M. Goliath is on exhibition at Div. Hdqtrs.
Issued by runners at 1,600 hours to:-
   The Philistines, for reflection.
   Mrs. Goliath, with deepest sympathy.
   Wills' Munitions (B.C.) Ltd. with testimonial regarding products.

When Elias Greener went on leave he got married - to a twin. Then it was known that the twins were sisters, and the boys asked Elias how he could tell which was which.

"Well," said Elias, "they're a nice family, you know, and I never bother very much."

August 19th, 1933

ONE DIRTY night in the fall of 1917 a rain-soaked, mud-laden, front-liner plodded along the Vlamertinghe road, going on leave. He was chilled to the bone and very weary. All at once he saw the door of a hut opened, and he headed toward the light. It was an Army Service Corps hut, and there was a good fire in the big stove, but all space around it was occupied by the A.S.C. lads who made no move to let the front-liner get near. So he stood in the rim of the outer group, listening to stories about dreams, and one smart lad, spotting him, said: "You, Jock. Did you ever have a queer dream?"

"I did-last night," said Jock gloomily. "I dreamt I died and went to Hell."

"Ah-now." There was a chorus of exclamations. "And what was it like?"

"Just like here," returned Jock bitterly. "A big fire, crowded with A.S.C. blokes."

When I was up in "Plugsteert" on my visit to the old war areas, I saw a hard-bitten old lad enter an estaminet, and I followed him in. He ordered beer. The stout proprietor brought it, and stood, rubbing his hands, trying to be friendly though he got little encouragement.

The customer drained his glass, and, as a last effort, the proprietor said: "Dark, isn't it? It looks like rain."

"Yes," said the hard-bitten one wearily, "and it tastes like it, too."

There were three brothers in Melbourne, Australia - Maurice, Richard and Sidney Crawcour. They all enlisted. Maurice lost his left leg at Anzac on Nov. 14th, 1915. Richard lost his right leg on the Menin Road in September, 1917. Sidney lost his right leg in Nov., 1917, during an action in the Gueudecourt sector.

In the Talbot House at Poperinghe, during the war, a young officer, looking for writing material, came across a dirty looking transport driver writing a letter home. The officer stared at him.

"Haven't we met before?" he asked.

"Yes, sir," said the private.

"By Jove, I have it," said the officer. "You were one of my professors in mathematics up at Oxford."

"Yes, sir," replied the private, "and I'm still looking after mules."

WHAT DID I GAIN FROM MY WAR SERVICE?

(from *The Listening* Post).

"A lad in his early twenties asked me what I gained from nearly four years of front line service.

Looking back, I see an irresponsible, hasty-tempered lad of twenty-one going to war largely for the fun of the thing. First came intense training, with discipline, which taught me I was a very minor unit - only a splinter in the spoke of a wheel. It taught me true humility and the worth of respect and obedience. From bitter experience I learned self-control.

Then came the battle years, the hell of which taught me to get a little closer to someone's side. I learned to appreciate humanity. Other men taught me to be cheerful in the face of adversity.

I spent three months in hospital, and there I learned the lesson of courage. There I saw the spirit which could face pain, maimed limbs, sightless eyes and unhearing ears with a courage mixed with kindness and self-forgetfulness.

I discovered :

That because a man appeared to be hard-boiled was no evidence that he did not possess a heart of gold.

That in motive, most profanity is an offence against good taste, rather than a sin against the Deity, and that many virtuous men have foul mouths.

That essential gentlemanliness is as apt to be found in the cook's son as in that of the earl's.

That intelligence is not confined to men of academic training.

That there "is so much good in the worst of us, and so much bad in the best of us. . . ."

The most vital thing which came out my war service is that immortal comradeship which grew big when there were no such petty things to divide us as capital and labor, creed or color.

Though bleeding and torn, a new man was born in the din of the warring thunder.

"I am a better man, please God, because of the things I got out of war."

When Paddy Flynn went to London on leave he was warned to be careful in getting about by taxi cab. One evening, however, he had celebrated so well that he could not walk back to his hostel, and summoned a taxi. Getting in, after much difficulty, he settled back on the cushions, and the driver had considerable trouble in learning his destination. He started the car abruptly and Paddy tumbled forward against the door, which had been left unlatched, and fell out on the street. Clambering up to the side of the car, Paddy said. "That's fast work, me lad. How much do I owe yez?"

When Gallipoli was evacuated there was a considerable amount of bombs and ammunition at the front trenches which could not be taken away, yet it was desired that these did not fall into Turkish hands. So a grave was dug,- a deep one, and the bombs, etc., heaped therein. Then all was covered and a decent mound made on which was placed a cross with the following inscription:

To the Memory of
PTE. BULLET
R.I.P.

The Turks were puzzled by the manner in which the British had taken away all bomb supplies, but no one thought of disturbing the resting place of "Pte. Bullet."

Survivors of the First Contingent of the New Zealand Rifles, which took part in the South African War, just number 117. They held a reunion this year, and, after the loyal toast, gave their war cry, which was, "Ake, Ake, Kia Kaha,Hautana Auahiana."

August 26th, 1933

REMEMBER THOSE deep dugouts in the railway embankment near Lens. One day a staff officer came up in that locality. All was very peaceful-until four pip emma. Then Fritz did his daily stunt. He dumped a couple of lorry-loads of whizz-bangs in and around the curve of the embankment. The red tabs plunged for the nearest underground, and descended like an avalanche, nearly killing himself and those below. When revived he was very ugly. "I'm going to report this place," he gritted between groans. "You should have a decent stairway here."

"We have, sir," managed the sergeant in charge," but you-you came down the chimney."

A few months ago there met in Geneva a great company of disabled veterans of most of the countries that fought in the World War. Arthur Henderson, president of the Disarmament Conference, addressed them, and in the course of his speech told them this story:

"There is a little English village-too small to get on the map. When war broke out in 1914 this village had just 19 boys of military age, and every one of them enlisted. Every lad was killed in action. The village was so stirred that it determined on a suitable memorial, but had so little money that it accepted a German field piece and placed it on their central green. On one side of the carriage a tribute is inscribed to the gallant nineteen who died. On the other side is engraved the name of the British company who first sold this gun to the Germans with which British youths-like the nineteen of the village - were mown down."

How We Won the War,

by Bombardier (in the Passing *Show*).

At a certain base in France there was an Acting Unpaid Lance-Corporal who invariably managed to evade the daily drafts that went up the line, and, as far as as is known by the writer, succeeded in doing so until "Duration."

At the time of our introduction he had been three years in France. Previously he had "swung it" in Blighty; and, realizing that the Base represented the last stage of that long, long trail which ends in shell holes and barbed wire, he donned his thinking cap and prepared his supreme effort.

Through an announcement on the Order Board to the effect that a clerk was required in the Company Sergeant-Major's office he managed to eke out a precarious month, then came the sad day when the C.S.M. told him he was to be relieved and unless he had other employment must go up the line.

The Lance-Corporal took stock. He had no trade, but he had once played a cornet. Yet. . . . there was no band. . . . .

That evening he stood by the C.S.M. as the draft marched out. "Pity we haven't a band to play them out," he said. "The Dashires have one and the Blankshires, but these poor devils get no music."

"Yes," said the C.S.M. "We could do with a band."

The Regimental Sergeant-Major appeared.

"We were just saying," said the Lance-Jack, "that's it's a pity we have no band "

"That's so," agreed the R.S.M.

In the canteen that night the Lance-Jack met a man who had been a bandmaster, and he talked busily. Next morning he went to the R.S.M.

"I've found a man who used to be a bandmaster " he said. "And you know what we said about a band...."

"I don't want to see him," snapped the R.S.M.

"Thank you, sir," said the Lance-Jack. He went out and met his man. "It's all right," he said. "I'm to take you to see him this afternoon. Ever conducted a band in St Leonard's?"

"No," said the man, "but I know the town."

"Good enough," came the response. "You can say you ran a band there."

That afternoon they went to the R.S.M.. "This is the man," said the Lance-Jack.

"He. . . ."

"What the blazes!" roared the R.S.M.

". . . . used to have the band in St. Leonard's."

"Do you know the `Rose and Turkey?' " asked the R.S.M.

"Of course," said the bandsman.

Then the Lance-Jack went out and found a trombonist and a man who played the French horn. He reported to the C.S.M. "I've found two fellows for the brass band."

"What brass band?"

"The R.S.M. is talking of forming one."

"Then I better see about them," said the C.S.M., and he went to the Orderly Room. "I have two men for the band," he said.

"What band?" asked the clerk.

"Why, didn't you know they were forming one?"

"No," said the clerk, "but I'll ask the Adjutant."

"It's the first I've heard of it," said the Adjutant, "but you keep the two men till I see the Colonel."

The Colonel came in. "I hear there's a bandmaster and some bandsmen at hand," he said. "I wish we had a band. . . ."

"Just what I was going to ask you about, sir," said the Adjutant.

"There would have to be authority," said the Colonel.

"Very well, sir," said the Adjutant.

One week later the band was formed, and the Lance-Jack was its first member.

It became the best brass band at the Base. The Colonel said he founded it. The Adjutant said it was his suggestion. The R.S.M. claimed the honor as his. The C.S.M. explained-on the side- that it was really he who started it.

Acting Unpaid Lance-Corporal Smith said nothing.

Chapter 9: September 1933

September 2nd, 1933

WHEN WE arrived in England Paddy Flynn found the "George and Dragon," near Witley Camp, a splendid place at which to ease his thirst. Then came a night when he arrived at the pub after closing time, and hammered at the door until a grim, angular, bony-faced woman appeared.

"Get from here, you," she hissed. "I'll call the police."

Paddy looked at her carefully, and at the sign overhead. "Go back in," he hiccoughed solemnly. "It's your partner, George, I want to see.

In Italy, 25 per cent of the British Expeditionary Force were non-combatant; the percentage was 36.94 in Salonica, 26.91 in Egypt, and 32.93 in Mesopotamia.

In 1914, 16.63 per cent of the B.E.F. in France were non-combatant. In 1915, the percentage was 17.64; in 1916, it was 15.51; in 1917, it was 22.30; in 1918, it had risen to 32.27.

On the 3rd of August, 1918, there was a total of 4,943 British, 1,388 Colonial and 842 American nurses and other women working for the Royal Army Medical Corps. Other women in France were :

Government Departments - 99
British Red Cross Society - 1,094
Queen Mary's Army Cross Society - 7,808
Y.M.C.A. - 571
Church Army - 77
Soldiers' Christian Association - 54
Salvation Army - 150
Other Institutions - 204
Total Women in France (Other than Nursing Sisters) - 10,057

THE FIRST SHOT OF THE GREAT WAR

(From the *Ypres* Times)

The honor of firing the first shot fired by the British Army in the Great War belongs to "C" Squadron of the Irish Dragoon Guards, commanded by Capt. C. B. Hornby. This was on August 22nd. The regiment disembarked at Boulogne on the 15th, and reached Haupmont on the 19th. Contact with the enemy had not been established, and "C" Squadron was sent forward for that purpose.

Information gained reported that the Germans were moving in large numbers southwards from Brussels. Early on the 22nd the squadron moved along the main road towards Soignies. Patrols came in contact with German scouts, and retreated in hope of luring the enemy. A number of German Uhlans came on cautiously.

An ambush was quickly prepared. Two squadrons of the regiment placed their horses in cover and made ready to open fire. The Uhlans came on at a distance, then halted and turned, and at that moment Cpl. Thomas fired the first shot of the war.

Hornby and his 1st Troop of "C" Squadron charged down the road after the flee-ing Uhlans, and though these were joined by a full squadron the flight continued until the Uhlans were reinforced, suddenly, by several troops of German Hussars. With drawn swords the Dragoons plunged at the heavy-weight German Cavalry. Hornby crossed weapons with a German officer and ran him through the neck, thereby gain-ing distinction of being the first British officer to draw blood. He was awarded the Distinguished Service Order for his gallantry. The Dragoons routed the enemy, killing many and taking so many prisoners that they needed aid in getting them all escorted to the rear.

September 9th, 1933

WHEN WE arrived in London on our first leave Sambo Brown was hungry for some candy. Every shop he explored had Fry's chocolate and dinky hard-boiled stuff that Sambo hated, so he kept looking. Off Vauxhall Bridge Road he saw a small shop and went in. The bell tinkled and a small miss of about ten years came forward. Sambo looked at the display of bullseyes, pinks and squares, and asked the price. The little girl had been staring intently and understanding came to her as she spotted the Maple Leaf badge.

"Oh, mums," she yelled excitedly. "There's colaonials in the shop. Ain't the penny goods tuppence?"

Billy Guild was keen on the old castles of Merrie England, and talked so much about one he'd seen near Durham that he induced Jimmy John to go with him on the next leave. Of special interest was the room in which the lady of the castle was stran-gled. Arrived, the guide took them around, and at last pointed out the room.

"But," protested Billy, "last year you told me that room over there was the one."

"Oh-aye," returned the solemn old fellow, "but this 'ere room were 'avin' repairs done.

There is at Thiepval, on the Somme, an Anglo-French cemetery. It has been com-menced since the Memorial was built, and is for the reception of bodies discovered on neighboring fields, and will contain an equal number of French and British graves.

For some time there has been much arguing about the right of relatives of the Glorious Dead to wear war medals, and a ruling has been given. It reads:

"Decorations and medals may only be worn by the individual upon whom they have been conferred, and in no case does the right to wear decorations and medals or their ribands, devolve upon a widow, parent, son or other relative when the recipient is dead."

Similarly, in cases where a posthumous award is made and the decoration or medal is handed to the deceased's next-of-kin, such decoration or medal may not be worn.

Special instructions modifying the above rule are issued, through the medium of the Press, in connection with the anniversary of Armistice Day, requesting those who avail themselves of the distinction of wearing, *on that day only* , the decorations and medals of their relatives who fell in the Great War, to wear them on their *right breast to* commemorate their dead, so that the living, to whom medals have been awarded, may retain their time-honored privilege of wearing them on the *left breast*.

One of the most wonderful Memorials existing today is in South Africa - a garden. It is in Worcester (Cape Province), a Garden of Remembrance, embowered in Church Square, in honor of the men of Worcester who lost their lives in the Great War. Hugo Naude, a painter, designed and made the garden and tends it daily. He has gathered every beautiful plant and shrub in Karoo and the uplands of South-west Africa, and as a result has a miracle of beauty. There is no formal decorative plan. It is a wonderland of rockeries, with red spear-pointed aloes keeping guard. To linger there is to glimpse the Arabian Nights and some dream-garden of a Rajah in a fairy tale. In all South Africa there is nothing that can compare with it.

The Non-Combatant Corps was established in April, 1916, with 203 members, and had an average monthly strength, up to Dec., 1918, of 2,375 of all ranks.

September 16th, 1933

WHEN WE were up at Passchendaele our little Cockney Joe was badly wounded and left lying out in No Man's Land over night. A dead Heinie was sprawled very near him so that they faced each other. Joe looked pitiful, as he was unable to move, but he looked up at once when the stretcher bearer found him, and pointed to the Fritz.

"Turn 'im over, will yer myte," he asked. "'E's got an 'orrible fice."

No one who goes to visit the old battlefields should miss seeing the war museums. There is one at Paris, one at Mons, one at Ypres, and, the best of all, at South Kensington, London. At South Kensington you'll see a replica of Vimy Ridge, complete in every detail. Each trench is shown, each dugout entrance, each of the craters, all the war ground from Lieven to Thelus. You'll see the first draft of the terms of Armistice, and Christmas post cards devised by those at the front, some of them very original. There are medals of all kinds, every one used by the Allied armies, all the uniforms, all recruiting signs, each sword and sabre.

There is an underground dressing station. The trench leads through battered war territory. You press a button on the side of the immense case and electric light shows the underground, with its stretcher cases ready to be taken out, the medical officer and his assistants, the piled equipment taken from the wounded, all very realistic. You see a huge mast periscope that the Germans used in the Hindenburg line, labels of all kinds used for the wounded. Then there are the various things sent through the mails by spies, messages in code in Bibles, newspapers, etc., and raw rubber sent in coffee, rubber in soap, in books, in photo frames.

You can see things the German at home was using the last year of the war-coffee made from burnt barley and dandelion roots, tobacco made from clover, boots made from wood and waterproof paper, paper used in clothing, even as lace. There are all the various forms of propaganda used by both sides, mostly messages sent by means of balloons or dropped from planes. Press a button and electric light reveals a dugout that was in Gavrelle. It is exact in reproduction, with a soldier sitting by a table waiting his turn to go on post. Mess tin and candle ends, bully, his gas mask, a ground sheet, blankets on the bunk, everything breathes the very air of a wartime dugout.

Every badge used by the British forces is there, all shells and fuses, all bayonets, all kinds of grenades, even to the "oyster" variety which were to be thrown by a device operated by eight springs. The signalling outfits are all there, flares and parachutes and rockets, pigeon carts, and revolvers and rifles of all calibre. There are five machines against the wall. You place a penny in the slot and turn the crank, and see the war again, soldiers on the march, cavalry crossing a stream, a tank advancing against barbed wire, all phases of an "over-the-top" attack. Then come the machine guns, tanks, all helmets and every form of body armor, and camouflage suits that were worn when there was new snow in the winter. There are bear traps that German scouts placed in No Man's Land, periscopes that were cunningly used in trees, barbed wire and stakes, and every form of club and weapon used by raiding parties.

The old sign boards are numerous. WIND DANGEROUS; BURY AVE; TO COURCELETTE; DEATH VALLEY; SUICIDE CORNER; KEEP TO TRENCH IN DAYLIGHT. Then you see entrenching tools, and stretchers, and S.R.D. (Service Rum, Diluted) jugs. There is a naval department containing all that is of interest to the man who fought on the sea, then many replicas of towns and villages. Ypres is there, very complete in its 1918 form and Festubert. There are miniature memorials, and a list tells you of the town restored, and by whom.

Miraumont was restored by Burnley.

Fricourt by Ipswich.

Guillemont by Hornsey.

Neuville Vitasse by Paddington.

Monchy-le-Preux by the Isle of Wight.

Cherisy by Mitcham.

Courcelette by Brighouse.

Neuville-St.Vaast by Newport.

Oppy by Kensington-upon-Hull.
Albert by Birmingham.
Bapaume by Sheffield.
Martinpuich by Southampton.
Lens by Cardiff.
Festubert by Southport.
Souchez by Kensington.

There is a bicycle with two seats, an arrangement whereby the pedallers worked a dynamo supplying power for a trench wireless. No doubt the Heinie who neglected to salute or shave were the ones who rode the bike. The different details from hospitals, the appliances used, make one's flesh creep. Then you see the trinkets, the souvenirs made by prisoners in German camps, candle holders made from Bovril tins, all kinds of carving, and purses, belts, etc., made from rat skins.

You can see all the photographs taken by the B.E.F., and pay books, identity discs, all pictures and paintings. These cover the walls of the gallery. Three of the best pictures are the old German line near Arras, the Menin Road, and a view of Lens. There are scores of things that were unusual, small inventions, from bath sprays for an officer's dugout to trip alarms that rang bells in No Man's Land. One could spend a week in the Museum and never get bored.

One night when Sergeant Taylor was "beered" the boys dressed an African in kilts and seated him in our hut. Taylor came in, blinked and stared, and blinked again. "Light another candle, boys," he grunted. "It's. . . . dark in here."

September 23rd, 1933

EARLY IN the war a very dutiful British officer in charge of a post deep in the heart of Africa received a wireless message from his chief.

"War declared. Arrest all enemy aliens in your district."

A few days later the chief received this communication :

"Have arrested seven Germans, three Belgians, four Spaniards, five Frenchmen, two Swedes and an American. Please inform me with whom we are at war."

SOME OF THE War Diaries make interesting reading, and give one an idea of the frayed nerves of the writer. The following is a choice page from an Eighth Brigade unit:

July 28. We had just issued instructions for a respect order of our 500-men working party when the chill voice of the Beer Emma over the wheezy phone advised of the working party being cancelled. `You will move by train tomorrow, where I know not, when I know not.

The evening was spent in preparation, anticipation and invention of rumors. First it was south we were bound, then rearward, then north, and finally to Russia. About

10 P.M. we were informed that our destination was Arneke and that we were to be moved by strategetic train. Well, what was to become of us? What is a strategetic train, and how can a train show strategy?

July 29. The G.O.C. Division and the G.O.C. Brigade were there to wish us bon voyage. The remainder of our Brigade stayed behind; in fact, so far as we know, the Canadian Corps and the whole of the dependable military world.

No, there is no brigade operation order attached. We move on pink signal, faith and forms. No one knew to whom we belonged, but no doubt some kind staff officer would claim us at our destination. The train did better than most troop trains in France. We travelled via St. Pol, Aire and St. Omer and reached Arneke about midnight. The R.T.O.- a very meek, pious, dyspeptic-looking, spectacled youth-- detrained us with the assistance of a still more promising one-pipped Town Major. We were told that we were in X Corps and that we would be billeted.

July 30. A very promising map, in two colors, a list of billets as long as your arm, and the freedom of the area were presented to the C.O. We were to move in the morning and the Town Major knew of a good field and a kind farmer, and we carried on to the field. We found a really hospitable farmer, who got out of bed, turned over his barn to the officers and tucked everyone away splendidly."

This was one of the Canadian battalions hurriedly moved to the Kemmel Sector and into the line in August 1st "to prepare the front for attack pending arrival of the Corps"-which was heading for Amiens on August 8th.

There is another item of interest in the diary of the 116th Battalion, dated sixteen years ago - Sept. 17th, 1917.

"3 A.M. Enemy opened barrage on our front line and Communication Trenches for about 50 minutes. One officer and 73 STURM TRUPPERS attempted a raid on our centre and left Coy. frontages. A few crept forward through the wire and entered "C" Company frontage in an empty bay at the junction of 12th Avenue C.T. They left the trench immediately, and it is believed that they captured Private Dewes of `B' Company who had been wounded by the barrage about daybreak. Cpl. Cox of `C' Coy. climbed over our parapet and captured a prisoner. Sergt Mason of `D' Coy. also captured a prisoner, but our Lewis gun killed him before he was brought in. The enemy evidently intended a large raid, as our scouts found mobile charges left in front of our trenches in the A.M. Casualties, 2 other ranks killed, 13 wounded, 1 missing."

Then, four entries this date, from Canadian Engineers' diary:

Sept. 23, 1915. Heavy gunfire continued down south. Weather remained fair and hot, but at night it rained, converting thick dust on roads into glutinous mud. General Turner took over from General Bulfin of the 28th Div., and the 2nd Canadian Division became responsible for the front from Wulverghem almost up to Vierstraat, with the 1st on the right and 17th British on the left. Sappers in camp improvised a shower bath, using a pump and a section of hose from one of the tool carts. Reports of a great victory have been received. British Battalions have captured Loos and the

Tower Bridge. Highlanders are in occupation of Hill 70 and have penetrated as far as Cite St.Auguste.

Sept. 23, 1916. Taking advantage of clear weather yesterday, the enemy hoisted observation balloons and pitched a shell into our horse lines killing 20 and wounding 7. At 3 A.M. this morning a shell fell into Kay's Dump among boxes of cordite. Flames spread to 18-pounder ammunition and to a supply of flares, illuminating the night. Sapper Motley was wounded in the arm and headed for the rear, visioning immaculate beds and lovely feminine attendants. (As a matter of fact, an over-worked hospital orderly dressed his wound and left him in a cow stable). Under an army order this date the shaving of the upper lip is henceforth permissible.

Sept. 23, 1917. Barring mist at dawn, visibility remained good. Both artilleries were active in the direction of Lens. An enemy plane crashed near Oppy. The air was chilly at night. The 22nd and 25th furnished another large work party to deepen and extend Actress Trench. The work was strafed by machine gun and artillery fire which also swept Avion at intervals. Two of the 22nd became casualties.

Sept. 23, 1918. Two officers were detailed to examine dugouts in Vis en Artois. Patrols from the 5th Brigade established outposts in the direction of Moeuvres. The big dugout with three entrances on Mercatel Ridge is in use as Corps Headquarters. Plenty of sunshine, but the nights are cool. Working party near Inchy Halte was deluged with blue and yellow cross gas, many becoming casualties.

September 30th, 1933

YOU'LL REMEMBER that in war time some of the lads were joined in matrimony when on leave-then forgot about it. When Sergteant Taylor was in London, on the way home a woman peered at his kilt and collar badges, and accosted him, showing him a photograph. "I married a boy with a kilt like yours," she said, "and I know there was a `C' on his badges. His name was Jim, and I want him."

Taylor took the photograph, and gazed earnestly. It was the likeness of a skinny, undersized, weasel-like person with a face like a baboon.

"Want him!" echoed Taylor in amazement.

"What for?"

Scapel, Sword and Stretcher is the title of a book by Colonel R.J. Blackham, D.D.M.S., Ninth Army Corps in France, and in it are extracts from letters received by the Ministry of Pensions. Some of these "howlers" are as follows:

"Any further inflamation you can give me about my bad leg would be leprecated."

"You ask me if I was born in Wedlock. No, I was born in a Kentish town. Should it make any difference?"

"In accordance with instructions at the Klinic (clinic) I had had fever and ague enclosed in an envelope."

"'You have changed my left leg into my right arm. Will it make any difference to my pension?"

"I am glad to tell you that my husband who was to attend Board next Friday died on Tuesday."

"If I don't get either a pension or work my wife will have to go on the streets and lead an immortal life."

"We have received yours truly. I served in Ireland and the Isle of Wight from 1915 to 1919 in answer to yours truly."

"Just a few lines to say owing to your delay sending my pension we have not a morsel of food in the house. Hoping you are the same."

"I have been in bed three weeks with Dr. Brown and don't get any better. Can I try Dr. Smith?"

Our Number Six Platoon had a good assortment of Campbells and MacPhersons, and the latter were a dignified line of leathery Scots. Came a new draft after Vimy ridge, and among them was a recruit with a rather hooked nose and stooped shoulders. Along came the mail orderly. "Letter for MacPherson," he said. "Not you Jock, or Donald, or Tom, or Bruce. It's something beginning with an "S." The clan looked gravely at each other and there was silence until the recruit spoke timidly. "If that name iss Samuel it iss mine."

Among Australian veterans the argument has ever been- which was the worst, France or Gallipoli? In much the same manner our veterans discuss the vileness of the Somme and Passchendale and draw comparisons. *Reveille*, the Australian veterans' magazine, contains a fine article on the subject, entitled: "Anzac and France: Some Comparisons, by C. Smith, 14th Battalion, A.I.F.

"In comparison of the dangers and hardships endured in France and Gallipoli, the scale certainly weighs heavily against Gallipoli. Roughly, the dangers and privations more pronounced at Gallipoli were as follows:

1. Sniping more frequent.
2. Shortage of water acute.
3. Vermin-infected clothing.
4. Failure to escape the nerve-racking shell-fire whether resting or fighting.
5. More and more heavier work on account of shortage of men.
6. Prevalence of Barcoo rot, typhoid, etc.
7. Inferior food.
8. No billets.
9. No leave granted.

Sniping probably caused as many casualties out of the line at Gallipoli as there was in the line. The rugged nature of the country enabled enemy snipers to creep around at night and snipe from the rear for weeks on end. Sniping of this description was practically unknown in France.

Shortage of water caused many deaths (especially among the wounded) and very much discomfort among the fit. The taste of the limited quantities was vile, being a blend of petrol and chloride of lime. Toward the finish of the campaign this was not so, but such conditions were almost unknown in France.

The hot showers, together with the facilities of fumigating and changing clothes in France were such that a Digger had nobody but himself to blame for the presence of body lice. Soap and water were always available.

In France troops were withdrawn from the line after being in action to billets out of range of shell-fire. Not so in Gallipoli. Nights and days for months on end the troops were exposed to shell-fire, thus tending to lower their morale. The rugged nature of Gallipoli and the appalling losses from snipers required extensive trench systems being dug. The weakness of the units (numerically and physically) made it imperative that each man work harder and longer than was necessary in France.

Barcoo rot was the direct result of a salt diet, caused through eating tinned food and was unknown in France. Dysentery was also prevalent to an alarming extent on the Peninsula. During the first five months the men, when out of the line, had to prepare their own food. It consisted of bully, bacon, tea and biscuits. Occasionally tinned vegetables were available. Bread, sugar, butter, fruit, vegetables and salt were unknown and money could not buy them.

Straw was always available in France and barns could be made comfortable. In Gallipoli men lived in burrows and open dugouts. Material for constructing proper shelters was not available. Leave was an unknown pleasure, while in France, Paris and Blighty leave was always a possibility.

In comparison, the enemy artillery did not shoot at night at Gallipoli, except for a stunt; there was no gas or tanks, and aeroplanes were few.

From *The Growler*, trench magazine issued by the 14th Battalion: "Statements derogatory to the characters of the Adjutant, the Transport Officer or the Quarter-master are especially welcome, and three months' free subscription given where the statement can be proved." This declaration was followed by the comment that it would be futile for any of the injured persons to institute actions for libel, since the editors were "broke" anyway.

War Books for the Veterans' Shelf

The Intelligence Service Within the Canadian Corps, by Hahn, is a splendid book for the veteran who wants to know what manner of work was done by those specialists we so often envied. Major J. E. Hahn, D.S.O., M.C., was on the staff of the 4th Canadian Division, and fully qualified to write on such a subject. His chapter, "Sources of Information," is most interesting and contains interviews of prisoners.

"February 10th, 1918. Preliminary Examination of Prisoner of 3rd Coy. 1 Batt. 1st Guard Reserve Regt., captured 10-2-'18 in N-14-A.

Method of Capture: Prisoner belonged to a patrol party of which he states 12-14 were wounded by M. G. fire, including himself. He lost his party and was captured by one of our own patrols.

Dispositions: One battalion holding front line. One battalion in support. One battalion at rest.

Reliability: Prisoner had been employed as a batman for some time and had only been sent into the line 6-7th Feb. He has, therefore, only vague knowledge of the front. Communicative, and apparently reliable. Prisoner was examined while on operating table awaiting the administration of anesthetics.

Support positions: In cellars in eastern extremity of Lens.

Rest Billets: Oignies.

Company trench strength : About 130-140.

Food: Very poor, particularly so last few weeks, probably due to precautions taken against anticipated shortage if strikes prolonged. States "fichtebearen" (pine cones) recently used for food. Prisoner does not appear ill-fed.

German offensive: There are many rumors of a coming attack, but little definite information.

Rheinland is full of troops, several Divisions having come from Russia. They are said to consist of mixed young and old classes with returned wounded. In the event of a German attack on this front the 1st Guard Reserve Division would probably remain in the Lens sector, but would not take part in the first assault.

Morale: Fair, Prisoner gives the impression of being "fed-up" and states that orders to attack British troops cause much grumbling, owing to our deadly fire. Minor revolts in other regiments heard of but not actually witnessed.

Harassing fire: Prisoner states this is very effective and shows a thorough knowledge of roads and traffic arrangements. Fire is so accurate that teams and wagons frequently have casualties, roads being shelled regularly each night.

Gas attacks: While in the same sector about one-fifth of the Division became casualties in September, 1917, and suffered rather heavily in gas attack in November. As British gas is very effective, men have been trained to blow into masks when adjusting them, as sufficient gas has been gathered in masks to kill.

October 26th, 1917, Preliminary examination of prisoner of the 5th Company, 3rd Bavarian Infantry Regt., 11th Bavarian Division, captured 26th Oct :

The 5th Company was the right company of the Battalion, along Flanders Second Stellung. All 4 companies in the line distributed in shell holes, each company frontage being 250 yards. Company had 2 heavy and 3 light M. G.'s and trench strength of 120. Prisoner states no supporting troops between trench and support position N.E. of Passchendale. Enemy relies on holding front line in strength, and M. G.'s of support, and the Marksmen Detachment distributed in depth between trench position and Passchendale. Patrols were organized to locate our artillery fire, and in the event of counter attack these men would serve as guides to take units through gaps in our fire. Meetcheele and Mosselmarkt not held by manned trench systems but defended by heavy machine guns. The greatest importance was attached to the Bellevue Spur, which was to be held at all costs, and which the battalion commander of the prisoner stated that must not under any consideration fall into our hands. Company suffered 90 casualties throughout the day and finally surrendered after being outflanked.

Prisoner thinks that every effort will be made to regain lost ground."

The following is an example of information elicited from our own men captured by the Germans: Information given by Sergt. and five other ranks of . . . Batt., "B" Coy., captured at midnight 14-9-18 on the Canal near to Sauchy-Cauchy while on patrol.

"Battalion consisted of the 1st, 2nd, 4th and 5th. The. . . . Batt. having been disbanded before leaving Canada. Pioneers apparently did not belong to the Division.

"Brigade consisted of the 1st, 2nd, 4th, and 27th and in the morning took part in the attack on Monchy, and reached the edge of the village, but was driven back by German counter-attack. The attack was repeated in the afternoon and objectives gained. Brigade was pulled back to Arras that afternoon.

On the 31st Aug. the Batt. had a short rest at Ruhe Nach Lattre, St. Quentin, moved back to Arras 2nd Sept, and stayed there until 5th Sept. At this time they marched to Chalk Pit, 3 or 4 miles east of Monchy. Stayed in this vicinity until 10th Sept., and on night of 11th relieved the. . . Batt. of the Brigade in the front line. Canadians did not think they would stay long in this sector. Rumor had it they would be relieved by English Division. Prisoners did not know how much of their Brigade was in the line. Prisoners did not see any American tanks.

"B" Company had 140-150 men and 5 officers.

Prisoners did not seem conversant with military matters. Their statements contradict themselves on many points and bring out little news.

One officer and 2 sergts. and 12 O.R.'s were sent out by "B" Coy. to establish location of German post on W. side of canal. The officer was supposed to have reconnoitred the way previously, but despite this the patrol came under machine gun fire of the post. Seven were taken prisoner of whom one died of wounds. The officer and the remainder of the party were killed.

Losses: In Monchy attack Batt. lost 50-60 O.R.'s.

Reinforcements: When at St. Quentin-about 150-age 20 to 40, chiefly conscripts.

Leave: Is not stopped. 4 men are allowed to go weekly to France and England. No leave to Canada.

In front line, row of posts are held by 15 or 20 men commanded by an officer having 1 or 2 Lewis Guns. Owing to numerous German snipers the men were strictly forbidden, during the day, to leave their posts.

In Arras they were sheltered in cellars which are connected underground and shell-proof.

Gas: Latterly the sector of the Batt. was subject to considerable gas shelling. Owing to the heavy wind there were not many casualties through gas. English gas masks give good protection. Names of Company Commanders and Officer Commanding given.

Morale: Apparently tired of war. The men do not hesitate to indicate that they were not sorry to be out of the war. They do not think the war will be decided on the field."

Major Hahn shows very emphatically how the troops could have assisted

Headquarters. At Len's a map was captured which showed the exact location of 24 heavy machine guns. This map was kept by a casualty until he reached hospital, when he showed it to someone who realized its importance, and then rushed it back to Corps. The day prior to its arrival the part of Lens indicated in the map had been attacked, and the 24 M.G.'s caused excessive casualties. Had their location been known, each one could have been destroyed by artillery fire or smothered by smoke bombs.

He shows examples of good patrolling. Extract from Fourth Canadian Divisional Summary, Feb. 3rd, 1918.

Patrols: Right Battalion. At 10.30 P.M. a fighting patrol of one officer, 6 scouts and 2 Lewis gunners with gun left our line through gap in railway embankment, along sewer to within 20 yards of enemy outpost, which was in sewer about 5 yards from embankment. Patrol was being put into formation to attack post when an enemy patrol of 4 men came out of it. When within 15 yards of our men order was given to fire. As soon as levers of bombs were loosed 3 men turned and ran; remaining German stayed to throw stick bomb. Five bombs dropped around him, and he jumped into a shell hole, then started to crawl back. It is certain that this man was a casualty. Another three bombs were thrown but party could not find the man, although search was made to the foot of the embankment. The officer and 1 scout then ran to the post and threw 2 Mills bombs into the opening, but no enemy was in sight. Our patrol returned. It is thought that a rifle is more effective than Mills bombs for patrol encounter. 18 bombs and half a pan of Lewis gun ammunition were expended. At 11.15 P.M. 1 N.C.O. and 3 men left our front line, and went along railway where they remained for two hours. Heard hammering and talking in enemy's line rear of embankment. Returned at 5.30 A.M. No enemy observed.

Left Battalion: At 8.45 P.M. 2 officers and 2 O.R.'s left our lines and proceeded east, then south. Returned at 10.30 P.M. At 6 P.M. 1 officer and 3 O.R.'s left our lines and proceeded east, then turned toward Alpacca Trench, in which direction they went about 80 yards. Nothing seen or heard."

He reports a raid by the 46th Battalion along the Railway Embankment at 5.45 A.M., Feb. 14th, 1918. 3 prisoners and 3 M.G.'s captured in vicinity of Cat Trench. Casualties were very light.

10th Brigade Report of Raid, Feb. 13th, 1917:

"46th Batt. Area: Enemy front line severely damaged. Trench 12 feet deep, containing very deep dugouts, apparently joined. A dressing station was found in this area.

50th Batt. Area: Found area inside quarry much cut up. Trench railway track destroyed. Two dugouts located and dealt with.

44th Batt. Area: Support line much damaged. Two large dugouts in parapet which were dealt with. Trench system to right of quarry had a large number of dugouts all of which were bombed. Trenches wide and deep but badly broken up by shell fire. Planks were used as trench mats.

47th Batt. Area: Trench behind craters found in excellent condition, deep and wide, and well revetted.

Prisoners: 52 in all, belonging to 11th Bavarian Reserve Regiment. Included one officer and 3 non-coms. Exceptionally good physique and very intelligent. 2 men formed part of Minnenwerfer crew. All wore cotton underclothing.

Estimated casualties, Enemy, 160. 3 officers killed during fighting and many N.C.O.'s. Does not include dead found in trenches. 41 dugouts bombed and destroyed, 16 being large ones. Snipers' post and M.G. emplacement destroyed by Sappers. Two mine shafts blown by Sapper party, 3 more by party 176th Tunnelling Coy., all in area behind crater group."

Major Hahn's book gives remarkable insight into the value of good patrol work and observation posts. The British Intelligence Staff learned late in the war, that the best method for getting accurate information from a prisoner was to lead him to a telephone as soon as he was captured. Invariably, he would give fuller and truer detail when questioned in that manner.

Chapter 10: October 1933

October 7th, 1933

MEMBERS OF a certain aerodrome were wont to boast about the liquid capacity of one of their officers, a bulging major, while the followers of a major of the Engineers were sure that he was the champion "tanker" of the Canadian Corps. Things went on until a challenge was given and the rivals met one night in a drinking bout. Cherry brandy and the product of Haig & Haig were poured inward to join refreshments provided by the Vin sisters, until finally all liquors obtainable at the hour had been consumed. "How you feelin'?" demanded the airman thickly.

"Firs' rate," answered the Engineer. "Head's clear's bell."

The airman sighed. "Neither drunk" he murmured. "Might's well go home. I'm clear's a bell too."

They went out to their car and they climbed in. "Well," said the Engineer presently, "why don't you start?"

"I will," answered the airman profanely, "as soon as I find the.., blistered wheel." Thereupon they groped until they fell asleep. Both were in the back seat.

At the conclusion of the war 1,500 men were blind as a result of war injuries. Now, fifteen years after the war, more than five hundred others have lost their sight through the effects of gas poisoning or wounds. Over 30,000 men were discharged from the Forces suffering from partial loss of sight.

"THE ACE", the splendid German play now being produced in London, has real soldier actors. Raymond Massey, who takes the principal part of the German, Jurt von Hagen, was a captain in the Canadian Field Artillery from 1915 to 1916, was seriously wounded in France in 1916, and served in the Siberian campaign before he came to the stage, through the Oxford University Dramatic Society. Franklyn Bellamy was actually a British pilot in France from 1914 to 1918, and Wilfred Lawson, at the age of eighteen, was flying on the Western Front; he plays a German Infantryman in "The Ace." Esme Percy, who takes the part of a war correspondent, was in the Highland Light Infantry from 1916 onwards, and remained abroad with the Rhine Army until 1923, producing plays.

"The Ace" is a strongly dramatic play, and depicts the fear which attacks the great flying officer as the years of the war roll on.

Sergeant John Ripley, of the lst Battalion, Black Watch, was the first man of "Kitchener's Army" to win the Victoria Cross, and he was 48 years of age when he climbed on the enemy's parapet at Rue du Bois on May 9th, 1915, and directed his comrades to gaps in the German wire. He died last month.

The Twenty-First Battalion Communique, official publication of the 21st Battalion Clubs and Association carries some splendid details of wartime experiences, and is one of the finest papers of its kind in existence. Its mid-summer number contains the experiences of Private L.A. Hamilton, a signaller, on the night of March 3, 1918. The battalion had just relieved the 19th in the line about Lieven when there came a sudden increase of shell-fire. This became a steady roar and Hamilton and his chum realized that they were enclosed in a box barrage, meaning they were to be raided.

The Company was new to that part of the line, and all rifles and machine guns seemed strangely quiet. Then a sergeant raced along the trench shouting "Get under cover, Fritz is BEHIND us." The two signallers were at a rather isolated part of the front line, cut off completely from Headquarters Company, and a husky Heinie suddenly appeared in their rear and swung a "potato masher" at them. They dived into a small tunnel as the bomb exploded very near them; and trained the rifle they had seized on the entrance, ready to shoot any intruder. The Fritz shouted for them to come out or be blown to atoms, and they sat tight. He hurled a bomb in but it did not quite reach them and they were not damaged. He shouted again and they made no answer. Then a German officer came along and called in perfect English, "Well, boys, want to come out?" "Where to?" "Back with us. We'll give you a safe conduct back of the lines and the war will be over for you." "What if we don't come out?" "No hard feelings--we want prisoners. It's a chance for you to get out of this mess until the war is over." "No, thanks."

And the officer went away and left them there.

The Germans did not get a prisoner and had many casualties. The 21st lost four killed and a number wounded. The raiding party was 250 strong and they moved swiftly, but met most strenuous opposition from every man they encountered. Why the German officer did not attempt to further bomb or shoot the trapped men will never be known.

Australia has, to date, the following published volumes of her official history. Dr.C.E.W. Bean, Australia's famous historian, has achieved remarkable work. No person can find words adequate to describe our lack of such a history. The following are the various volumes of Australia's series:

Vol. I - *The Story of Anzac.*
Vol. II - *The Story of Anzac.*
Vol. III - *The A.I.F. in France*, 1916
Vol. IV - *The A.I.F. in France*, 1917.
Vol. VII - *The A.I.F. in Sinai and Palestine.*
Vol. VIII - *Australian Flying Corps.*
Vol. IX - *The Royal Australian Navy* .
Vol. XII - *The Photographic Record of the War.*

To be published:
Vol. V - *The German Offensive*, 1918.
Vol. VI - *The Allied Offensive*, 1918.
Vol. XI - *The War Effort in Australia.*
The full completed work of Twelve Official Volumes will be available before the end of 1936. Contrast that with Canada.

From *The Listening Post*, 7th Battalion war magazine :
"Wanted-Work wanted for several hundred able-bodied men at present employed only 20 hours each day. Would like profitable employment for remaining 4 hours. Digging or carrying preferred. Apply. . . . 7th Battalion."

October 14th, 1933

WHO AMONG those present can ever forget the Yorks and Lancs outfit that was billeted somewhere near Auchel - I forget the name of the village - and who held a grand inspection on a day that the Forty-twas marched through? One hard-head among them had been on a night's celebration and, in the morning, could not find his trousers. Someone had taken them, leaving in their place a pair of white canvas "bags." Around came the sergeant in the midst of a frantic searching, ordering every one to fall in, and he would not listen to any reasoning. Behold, then, before anything could be done, the deprived one appeared on the parade ground, front rank of the leading company, in those awful "bags." We witnessed three red-tabbed monsters shouting to high heaven, saw a file of huskies seize the offender and bear him off, no doubt, to an 'orrible fyte."

Which brings me to a strange incident I uncovered in records of the Yorks. and Lancs. Private Horgan was a member of the 7th Battalion and loved his rum issue above all else in France or Belgium. It was a dark, slushy night in the salient, and Heinie was paying particular attention to the region round about Hooge. There was a post west of the spot constructed in the reverse slope of the Ypres-Roulers railway embankment, a post consisting of deep saps and shelters with no visible exit or approach. Machine gunners inhabited the place, and rations were taken up them twice weekly upon an old railway bogie from Shrapnel Corner to a point near their position. As a rule two of the gunners came to the spot to meet the ration party, but on one occasion they did not appear and the N.C.O. in charge told Private Horgan to push the bogie on up to their position until he was challenged.

This was hard work, and the night was very dark and discouraging, so after a time Horgan decided he needed a rest, and during his breather came to the conclusion that he also needed help from the gunners. They had been shelled hotly during the evening, and the two to meet the rations were making their way by a long and difficult detour. Horgan realized that he was taking a chance in leaving the rations until he returned, so resolved to take the precious rum jug along. And that led him to consider himself entitled to a drink and also a few drops to put in his water bottle.

By the time he had reached a barbed wire barricade after much tripping and blundering in the darkness, he was rather incensed at the delinquent gunners, and a few odd drinks were required. He floundered in the wire and heard a voice somewhere near, saying, "halt." Horgan was no "halter." He kept on, and there came a burst of machine gun fire from the place where the voice had spoken-which made him move faster. He came to a second lot of wire, and got through it. And the next morning Private Horgan was reported "missing."

One week later there was unusual liveliness in the neighbourhood of Hooge Crater. Just before dark, in the last fading light, a man was observed to leap out of the German front line, plunge into a large hole under the wire entanglements, and then dash toward and into the British trench. He was pounced upon at once, for he had moved so swiftly and expertly that he was uninjured. He was dressed in Bavarian blue, with regimental numbers on his shoulder straps, roofed with a picturesque pot helmet, and armed with a long-barrelled rifle. His arrival was followed by intense bombing, shooting and shelling, but the deserter escaped it as he was well on his way to headquarters under strong escort.

The interpreter mustered his German and asked the prisoner's name - and was vastly shocked to be informed curtly that it was Private Thomas Horgan of the Yorks and Lancs.

He had gotten among the German outposts without being wounded, had imbibed freely from his rum jug, and slept. Near morning he had aroused, to hear German being spoken very close to his shell hole. In the next crater was a dead Bavarian, so Horgan slipped over and exchanged uniforms. For seven days he existed in the German outpost line grunting guttural answers when a furtive individual brought him water and rations, lying low during the daytime, sole occupant of a strongly-wired sap. An insistent call on the seventh evening caused him to join the outgoing sentries, but he changed his decision at a fork in the trench, and raced away to the front again. Arrived there he did not hesitate, but leaped out and over in the manner described. After such an adventure he was installed as a clerk in the Q.M.'s Stores and entirely cured of his weakness for rum.

"If you can drink the beer the Belgians sell you,
    And pay the price they ask with ne'er a grouse,
If you believe the tales that some will tell you,
    And live in mud with ground sheet for a house;
If you can flounder through a C.T. nightly,
    That's three parts full of mud and filth and slime,
Bite back the oaths and keep your jaw shut tightly,
    While inwardly you're cursing all the time ;
If you can grin at last when handing over,

And finish well what you had well begun,
And think a muddy ditch a bed of clover,
    You'll be a soldier one day, then, my son."
                                    - from the Wipers Times.

October 21st, 1933

Every Canadian veteran knows the story of the platoons of the 13th that fought to a finish in the Second Battle of Ypres, and there were many like episodes on a smaller scale before the war ended, yet there are not many readers who know that such heroism was grandly duplicated many times by the "Imperial" forces. I was especially impressed by such records when studying the accounts of the fighting around Cambrai. Two officers of the 17th Battalion, Royal Fusiliers, with a single platoon stemmed a German attack on Nov. 30th, 1917, until the remainder of their unit had made good their retirement and every man fought to the last. Not one survived.

A company of the 13th Battalion, Essex Regiment was cut off. They fought all the afternoon so desperately that the enemy was held in check; then came the dusk. The surviving officer and his sergeants held a consultation, and all voted against surrender. Two men were ordered to get through with a message to battalion headquarters, and the rest fought on. At sunrise not one remained alive.

Near Ville-aux-Bois-les-Pontavert, by the side of the main highway leading from Laon to Rheims, there stands a simple memorial to the 2nd Battalion of the Devonshire Regiment, and it carries a story of bravery that has seldom been equalled in history. The story is a quotation from an Order of the Day, published by General Berthelot, who commanded the French Fifth Army, and under whose orders the Devonshire men served. The inscription runs:

"On the 27th May, at a time when the British trenches were subjected to fierce attack, the Second Battalion Devonshire Regiment repelled successive enemy assaults with gallantry and determination, and maintained an unbroken front until a late hour. The staunchness of this battalion permitted defences south of the Aisne to be organized and their occupation by reinforcements completed.

Inspired by the sang-froid of the gallant commander, Lieutenant-Colonel R.H. Anderson-Morshead, D.S.O., in the face of an intense bombardment, the few survivors of the battalion, though isolated and without hope of assistance, held to their trenches north of the river and fought to the last, with an unhesitating obedience to orders.

Thus the whole battalion, Colonel, 28 officers, 552 N.C.O.s and men responded with one accord and offered their lives in an ungrudging sacrifice to the sacred cause of the Allies.

(Signed), Berthelot,
        General Commanding 5th Army."

Writing of such memorials reminds me of Le Quesnoy, a small fortified town, one of the most picturesque places in Europe. It is a quaint, old-fashioned centre with more than a touch of mediaeval times about its carved fronts and peep-hole windows and gabled roofs, and is entirely surrounded by an earthworks that was considered impregnable before the war. There is German wire still clinging in obscure places on the massive walls, and adorning various gates by which you enter the town. The streets have war names, "Avenue d'Honneur," and Rue du Marechal Joffre," etc. Walk around the grassy ramparts and one comes to a beautiful garden at the end of which is a deep moat. There is a long railing and the wall of brick is fully thirty feet high. It is scarred and dented deeply by shell fire, and in among those scars I found a plaque that explains the park-like surroundings. It is all a memorial to the New Zealanders.

"From the uttermost ends of the Earth" is the inscription on a seat overlooking the tablet, and the tablet bears a scene showing the New Zealanders swarming up a ladder placed at the actual point the plaque indicates. Their feat in a most dashing assault was probably not duplicated during the war, as one has only to see the wall to realize the desperate valor required for such an enterprise.

A new padre came to us, and Sunday morning visited the hut and asked for men to "join the righteous army." Three newcomers left their bunks and went forward. "Ah," said the padre "What is your religion?" Baptists, sir." "There " piped up Paddy Flynn, "ye'll have to put thim in your Navy."

Until October, 1916, only the small photographic equipment of the Royal Flying Corps was used for reproduction. Then the aeroplane photography made such demands that the Army Printing and Stationery Services Photographic Section was opened for the Fourth Army, equipped to produce 5,000 whole-plate prints daily. It was so successful that a similar section was given each Army, and the photographic work was extended to mosaics, panoramas, maps, stereoscopic photographs for operations, reproduction of all Graves Registration photographs, photographs of deserters and escaped prisoners, and general outdoor photography for training or record purposes.

The number of photographs taken or reproduced grew as follows:

1916	25,000
1917	2,095,750
1918 (to October)	2,244,750

At the end of 1915, when the Canadians held the line between Voormezeele and Ploegsteert, the rains combined with the German shelling to make the trenches unfit and the men's lives miserable. Parapets fell in or were blown in, shelters were flooded and sickness thinned the ranks. The general conditions were vastly depressing, but this is how one trench magazine re-acted :

"Extracts from (expected) Brigade Orders.

l. Commanders of submarines plying in the communication trenches are requested to see that these vessels are not used by pleasure parties between the lines.

2. Non-commissioned officers and men are not allowed to use the bathing beach at XZ-50 Trench. This is for officers only.

3. Ration and fatigue parties must not participate in swimming races to the firing line owing to the presence of hostile submarines.

4. Owing to the scarcity of material for filling sand bags, any man who consumes more than 10 lbs. of mud per day will be severely dealt with."

"It has been demonstrated that a bullet which will penetrate 18 inches of solid brick-work, will pierce only 1-1/2 inches of bread (army issue)."

Paddy Flynn, while in the Quarry Line, was sentenced to dig a sizable latrine, and not to return to the dugout until it was finished. The spot chosen was a rubbish-filled cellar. Shortly after, a soldier passing saw what appeared to be a cave-in, and Paddy's steel helmet was partly buried. A hurried digging party ensued, and finally the whole place was cleared-but no Paddy. Then he suddenly appeared from the hiding of another ruin.

"Thank ye, kindly," he grinned. "'Tis a hard job it would have been to dig all of that mesilf. I'll never forgit ye while I'm sober."

The language that followed almost caused the earth to heave and fill the cellar again.

War Books for the Veteran's Shelf

Through Hell to Victory, by Reginald A. Colwell. It is a story of the 2nd Devons, and has one of the most vivid descriptions of the mud at Passchendale that I have read. The author served with his unit the last year of the war, and was first at Passchendale in January 1918.

Here are selections from his story: "Brandhoek was their first stop. The chief charm of Brandhoek was the road. It was no ordinary road. It was the main artery through which flowed the life-blood of those poor devils freezing in the mud and in the shell holes before Passchendale and around it.

Along it went all stores, all the men, all the guns, all the food, all the ammunition-everything. Night and day, year in, year out, the procession of men, waggons, lorries and guns went on, and on, and on, and on. The enemy shelled and bombed the road. Yet the military policemen stood there on point duty, regulating the traffic, for twenty-four hours every day. At night a dim, shaded storm lantern showed where they stood.

There were corners where horses passed at a gallop, and men "doubled." Every now and then there were shells pitching on the road, creating awful carnage. But the traffic must not stop. If a motor lorry could not be started in two minutes it had to go. If it could not be pushed out of the way every man available was called on and it was toppled bodily into the ditch. If a shell knocked out two or three waggons and tore a great hole in the road, the waggons and all there was in them were buried in it, and the earth thrown in by everybody who could lift a shovel. And the traffic moved again-always on, on, towards those greedy guns which forever called for shells or fodder.

Yet there was something wonderful, something fascinating about this road. There was magic in the grinding wheels and the steady tramp of feet. Many thousands only went one way on this road. They went up, but they never came back.

On Thursday, January 3rd, 1918, a night of bright moonlight and hard frost, the battalion went into the line proper.

The weather was hard. All the shell holes were frozen over; the swamps were impassable. It was difficult to walk that night. Some tied sandbags around their feet to get a foothold. Laden like pack mules, they slipt and fell all over the place. Hardly a section got through with its rum jar unbroken. It was a bad start for the New Year.

So they struggled on with their heavy burdens. They carried picks and shovels for trench digging, although, when they arrived, they found half a dozen picks and shovels for every man. And they knew, as the authorities must have known, that they would not be able to use them. Nothing short of dynamite would have broken that hard frozen ground.

At that time there were no trenches, and there was no wire. The line was a line of posts. Just a few men in enlarged shell holes. In some places they had been connected up for a few yards. There they stayed, keeping doubled up all day. The Germans, sometimes only ten yards away, were in as bad a plight. There was no fighting. It was a question of watching and keeping low all day.

The artillery on both sides kept busy all the time, particularly at night, and the German machine guns were sources of as grave discomfort to us as ours were to them.

At night the guns made merry. The whole earth shook in the constant barrages all round, Our aeroplanes went over and the German aeroplanes came back. The ration parties and fatigue parties suffered heavily, for they had no protection. The enemy had the range of the duckboard tracks and, night after night, he raked them with machine gun fire and shelled them with shrapnel. Day and night he poured gas shells over the sunken road behind Bellevue. Every night he knocked down the wireless mast on the pillbox on the hill at Bellevue. And every morning we put up a nice, new white pole.

Then came the thaw.

Under the hill at Bellevue a mineshaft had been dug. In it were constructed offices and places in which were wire-netting beds, like bunks in a ship, and if you went there you could see men off duty stretched out on those mattresses. From above the water poured as from a tap. It ran off the waterproof sheets of the men on the top deck on the men who filled the lower bunks. Pumps were always going but the water was over your boots all the time.

There were, scattered about, a few alleged places as shelters, but they were only bits of corrugated iron covered with earth. They afforded no protection, even from rifle bullets, and hardly kept out the rain. For the most part the men crouched in their small holes, sitting in mud and water, happy only in the knowledge that the enemy was as badly off.

There was a sort of sympathetic tolerance on both sides. It was even whispered that two posts opposite each other made signs not to fire. Then they crawled out and danced about to warm their half-frozen feet.

When the thaw came no pen could tell of its awfulness. No painting, no photograph, no description, however vivid, will bring home to anyone who did not see it more than a glimmering of an idea of what it was like.

Down on the Somme there were real houses, with roofs in some cases. The trees had green leaves on them for some part of the year, though their branches may have been broken and torn by the shells. The birds sang above the barrage and sweet flowers managed to exist in the fields.

Here, all was different. For miles and miles there was not a sign of life of any sort. Not a tree, save a few dead stumps which looked strange in the moonlight. Not a bird; not even a rat or a blade of grass. Nature was as dead as those Canadians whose bodies remained where they had fallen the previous autumn.

Death was written large everywhere. Where there had been farms there was not a stick or stone to show. You only knew them because they were marked on the map. The earth had been churned and re-churned. It was simply a soft, sloppy mess, into which you sank up to the neck if you slipped from the duckboard tracks and the enemy had range of every foot of those slippery ways.

Shell hole cut across shell hole. Pits of earth, like simmering fat, brimful of water and slimy mud, mile after mile as far as the eye could see. It is not possible to set down the things that could be written of the Salient. They would haunt your dreams. "The worst front in the war, " said the men who had been on most fronts. - It was.

In 1914, 626 horses and 20 mules were lost at sea during the voyage from North America to the Western front. In 1915, the loss was 3,865 horses and 2,819 mules, which includes 834 sunk, 26 killed by shell fire, and 23 mules killed in the same manner. In 1916, 699 horses were lost at sea, including 300 sunk, and 252 mules were lost. In 1917, 3,318 horses were lost, including 2,732 sunk, and 451 mules were lost, including 200 sunk and 14 killed by shell fire. In 1918,1,248 horses were lost at sea, including 881 sunk, and 426 mules, including 258 sunk.

October 28th, 1933

OUR QUARTER-BLOKE was very partial towards Scotch whiskey and the liquids obtainable in France. When things were going well with him he was in a delightful state for days at a time. There came our visit to Bourecq, and while there the old lad lost his way one dark night and fell into the canal. A crony of his from the transport section reported the action after he had pulled the old boy to shore.

"Jock's not drooned, ye ken," he repeated solemnly, after many hiccoughs, "but he's *badly diluted.*"

"Mousetrap Farm," in the Salient was merely marked "Chateau" on Belgian war maps, as "Chateau du Nord " on French ones, and as "Shell Trap Farm" on British ones, until a Corps order named it to all as "Mousetrap Farm."

St. Julien was a town of 191 houses before the war and had a population of 963. It is now the centre of the "pillbox" area, and 126 of its structures are memorials. The pill-boxes were made of ferro-concrete, reinforced with five-eight-inch round iron rods. Water-worn gravel was brought to the Salient by the Germans and used in their work, This was routed from the Rhine through Holland via the Meuse and Scheldt in barges and by rail, and pillboxes built from such material resisted direct hits by six-inch howitzers and artillery of even greater calibre.

There are concrete dugouts in the canal bank close to Essex Farm Cemetery in the Salient and others at Grune Farm and McDonald's Wood. There is a German brigade headquarters in St. Julien and another at Gheluvelt, and a British observation post inside the original farm buildings at Hussar Farm. It escaped destruction despite four years of enemy bombardment.

Near one of the pillboxes at Steenbeek crossing Capt. N. G. Chavasse, Victoria Cross, Military Cross, of the Royal Army Medical Corps won, on July 31st, 1917, a bar to his Victoria Cross, the only person to be awarded the unique decoration during the World War. While carrying a wounded man to his dressing station he was himself wounded on the right side of the head, but insisted in carrying on. He went repeated-ly with stretcher parties and brought back wounded from the firing line, and for two days continued the most heroic service. On the 2nd of August, in the morning, a shell pitched directly into his dressing station and he received a terrible wound in the body. He was at once taken to the field hospital at Brandhoek, but died on August 4th.

One of the strongest pillboxes in the Salient was the redoubtable "Cockcroft " near Triangle Farm. In 1917 it was a regular fortress, withstanding all shelling and defeat-ing two determined assaults by the 7th Worcestershires. Then the tanks were brought up, and one wallowed through the mud to within fifty yards of Cockcroft. The German garrison were astounded by its appearance and fled headlong. The platoon of British infantry following the tank occupied the stronghold without suffering a casu-alty. At Triangle Farm itself the 8th Worcestershires got to the blockhouse entrance and there engaged in a frightful battle of bayonets. Almost the entire garrison were killed by cold steel before the place yielded.

At Messines Ridge, after the mines were blown, a German pillbox was entered-and found to be occupied by the dead. Four German officers sat around a table where they had been playing cards, each man upright in his seat, his arms resting on the table. They had died without a mark of injury, their bodies rigid as metal.

Lumm Farm has a huge pillbox of several chambers, well worth visiting. This was attacked by the 15th Royal Irish Rifles, and their officer, as he plunged into the strong point, was grappled by the German major in charge. There ensued a terrific struggle as both were large, powerful men, but the Irishman finally wrenched an arm free at a critical moment and put his opponent out of action. This huge concrete shelter was used afterward as a dressing station by an Australian Field Ambulance.

We had just got a "Canadian mail" at Villers au Bois when a kit inspection was ordered. One of the cooks had been married just before leaving Canada, and was very interested in his letters. Around came Major Grimm, inspecting. "Razor- tooth brush-knife-" he said slowly as he peered, then he looked at the cook. "Housewife? " he barked.

"Fine, thanks," grinned cookie. "How's yours?'"

But he had nothing on our little Cockney Joe, who, rumor had it, was married to an immense, deep-voiced, frowsy-headed battle axe, a woman who ruled him with an iron hand. Joe was just back off leave when he fell in for parade. The sergeant passed along, glanced at him and dug him in the ribs.

"Button up yer tunic," he growled huskily.

"Yes-yes, my dear," said little Joe.

"And now I know," said Elias Greener, as he searched his seams in Goodman Tunnel, "why that guy Napoleon always had his picture taken with his hand in the front of his shirt."

Remember the way the transport men used to churn their harness and chains in sand bags to get them polished and glittering? I saw two Lancashire mates at such labor while their battery was out on rest, and they seemed fed-up.

"Tom, dost know what Ah'm goin' to do when war's o'er?" asked one.

"Noa."

"Ah'm goin't buy some of yon harness, hang 't in 't barn-and watch stoof rust."

We were marching to Divion, and Joe asked a native how far it was to Houdain.

"Five miles as de crow fly," came the surprising answer, and the native was proud of his English.

"But 'ow far," persisted Joe, "if the barmy bird 'as to 'op it?"

Chapter 11: November 1933

November 4th, 1933

"Said a Cockney on furlough from Ypres:
It's a rotten old village for snypres,
    And the things that they do
    Ain't exactly what you
Reads abaht over 'ome in the pypres."

"There was a young man at La Clytte,
Living where he had always wet fytte;
    He could drink up his ale,
    By the jug or the pail,
But he rarely, if ever, touched mytte."

"Cos I'm the Town Major of Loos,
The troops gimme lots of abuse,
    But you'll say at a pinch,
    It ain't any cinch
To be the Town Major of Loos."

These are from old Trench magazines which helped the lads at the front keep their mental equilibrium.

Remember the famous "barrier" on the Messines Road? In the *History of the 2nd Canadian Mounted Rifles* the writer deals with it candidly. "Early on the morning of the 3rd (December, '15) came a report to Battalion Headquarters from Major Bardolph that there was a new barrier of sandbags on the Messines Road about 150 yards from our line, where previously had been only two trees cut down by shell fire, and the remains of a house beside the road. These trees and the ruin had evidently been used for a long period by the Bosche as either an outpost or listening post, for on careful and patient observation through the glasses, a communication trench from the German front line could be traced to the road, and the ditch deepened along the road to the ruins. The sandbags were simply the natural result of our incessant harrowing fire along the road at nights. The consternation raised at Canadian Headquarters by this barrier was tremendous, quite out of proportion to the cause, and in the light of after events would have been ludicrous had it not resulted for some time afterward in great ill-feeling and many fights between certain units of the 1st Division and the C.M.R. Had we been allowed, as we were for raids in later days, to form our plans deliberately for the capture of the barrier we would have undoubtedly done away with it before our relief was due. But this was not to be; at 11 P.M. the same night, Brigadier-General Seeley's staff-captain, Captain Docherty, came in with a peremptory order from the general to the effect that we must attack and capture the barrier before dawn. This gave us no chance to send out patrols to scout the best way of approaching the objective; it didn't even give our bombers a chance to look at it over the parapet and so get some idea of what they would be up against. Under these circumstances, it was decided that the only thing to do was to make a frontal attack, by surprise, if possible, along the road, the probability being that the flanks would be protected by wire entanglements. Lieutenant N. Rant, scout officer, and Lieutenant A.V. Evans, bombing officer, were chosen to lead two parties of bombers and bayonet men, another party being detailed to support the attack should it prove successful. By dint of desperate effort, everything was arranged an hour before dawn and the attackers went over the top, Lieut. Rant with his party leading, with Lieut. Evans' party in close support. The Huns, however, were on the alert and commenced bombing before our men were in range; in spite of this, Rant and his men worked forward until stopped by wire barriers, and threw all their bombs, but failed to get through the wire. Lieut. Rant was blown into the ditch by the explosion of a Bosche bomb, and as soon as he got out was blown across the road and knocked silly by another bomb; Corporal J.W. Potts was also wounded. As they were now out of bombs and the Bosche defence seemed to be growing stronger, the balance of the squad withdrew, carrying their officer and the corporal. In the meantime Evans' squad had been trying to work off the road to outflank the objective, but owing to unfamiliarity with the ground, failed, and also withdrew after loosing off their grenades at the Hun. Nothing further could be attempted now as day was breaking and the Hun was getting busy with his artillery. We had, therefore, to report to brigade that the attack had been unsuccessful.

This lesson should have been sufficient, but was not. No regiment was allowed to formulate plans, but attack after attack was ordered by General Seely with the same haste, and carried out with the same lack of success as ours, until the disastrous one in which the Strathconas had many casualties, losing one officer and two other ranks, badly wounded, taken prisoners by the Huns.

The barrier was finally dealt with quite easily after the First Division took over the line and sane military policy prevailed. Plenty of time was allowed to work out a scheme, with the result that a field gun, which was manhandled up to the front line, one night at a given time, when a barrage was laid on the German front line, opened direct fire on the barrier for five minutes, knocked-it completely to pieces. A party of infantry then occupied the objective, finding little but ruins and dead bodies, and the gun was hauled back to safety almost before the Bosche realized what was happening."

Other accounts of this barrier will follow.

Do you know that the 4th Canadian Mounted Rifles had fourteen clergymen serving in their ranks?

Up on the Ypres-Vlamertinghe road one dark night in 1917 a driver had his horse killed, and his officer sent him back, with a chum, to bury the animal. While working they struck metal boxes, and opened one. It was filled with gold coins, too heavy to carry. The Germans began to strafe the road, and they hurriedly filled the cavity revealing the boxes, but a shell close by killed the chum and wounded the driver. It was a year before he got back, and he couldn't find the spot. He came back as soon as he was demobilized and began further search, and the Belgian police grew curious, then ordered him away. Today he is working in the Salient, driving a truck, and every month or so, when the night is dark and wet, he sneaks back and digs till daylight. But, in 1932 he hadn't found the treasure.

November 11th, 1933

"I wonder how you sleep today, my mates,
    So far away and out of reach or call;
Can there be more than mem'ry isolates
    Your portion now, beneath your grassy pall;
Hold you your rightful pride or do you rue your fates?
            I wonder-yes-I wonder.

I wonder if you think your lowly bed
    Warm comfort of that war-torn patient earth;
And do you feel those poppies ardent red
    A destiny that beckon'd you at birth;
Is there another symbol you would have instead
            I wonder-yes-I wonder.

I wonder if the battle filled your ears,
    Or can you hear the wind and rain, and song
Of skylarks, fluting to allay your fears;
    Hear you the strangers tread all the day long ;
The bugles at the Menin Gate like crystal tears?
            I wonder-yes-I wonder.

I wonder if you really Rest in Peace,
    And if at last you think you lost or won;
Does this 'leventh hour when all sounds cease
    Mean more to you than any morning's dawn;
I wonder if you could would you desire release?
            I wonder-yes-I wonder.

I wonder if you dream of leave, Dover
    And Blighty, or have you temporal bail

That makes of you an ethereal rover;
   Do flags mean anything beyond the veil?,
And what will be your shouts when I cross over?
     I wonder-yes-I wonder.

"THE YEARS PASS, THY MEMORY REMAINS." I saw the inscription, in French, on a headstone in a little war cemetery near Arras. And by questioning got details. It was another soldier lad who had fallen in love with a peasant girl, another boy the first time from home, yearning and hungry for love, and so they two of different tongues had met and understood each other. Then he had fallen and came no more back to the little village with its shop windows displaying chocolate and silken post-cards, its houses with billeting signs on doors and gateways. Thirteen long years had come and gone -and that peasant girl stays true, true to her memories.

Away down near Amiens as I lingered in a little wayside cemetery of scarce more than one hundred graves I saw a frail, bent, old woman coming in at the gate. She was lame and leaned heavily on her cane, yet seemed familiar. Then I knew. It was she who had her small paper stand near the railway station, and was there day in, day out , rain or shine, even on Sundays, endless hours on duty. She went her way, slow and painfully, to the iron box set in the wall where the register of graves was kept, and there she placed two francs. It was about ten cents in our money.

"Why," I asked the gardener, "does she do that?"

"It is to help pay for the looking after these graves," he said, removing his cap and speaking kindly as the old lady, after crossing herself and murmuring a prayer, was leaving again. "She barely makes a living selling a few papers, yet she scrimps and saves till she gets a few francs, and then walks away out here to put her money in that box. She says she can never forget the boys who fought to save her."

Fifteen years ago the bells were ringing and whistles blowing, and flags flying. The war was over!

Get the gallant boys back home. Greet them as never soldiers had been greeted before. They'd earned it. Four long years-and sixty thousand who didn't come back. The world was theirs', anything they wanted.

Ah. yes-fifteen years ago. . . .

Now thousands more are in graves on this side, dead while they should yet be young, and the others struggle to live, plead hopelessly with soul-less powers who renege their promises made, who grind these broken veterans to starvation, shame and suicide.

"The years pass, thy memory remains."

No country that keeps not true its pledged word given so freely as it sees dangers removed and freedom held, can hope to prosper. All may not be right with the world, but men are still their brother's keeper, and the land that keeps Cain in high places will never get right.

November 11th. There was no jubilation at the old front. We sat around and saw pictures-mud holes-faces-barbed wire stand-to-parapets- still forms under blankets-boots, worn and muddied boots, protruding from ambulances-pitiful khaki forms huddled on the bath mats. War. . . . We had seen War; and we had seen through it.

In a shattered ruin, in the one room left intact, three soldiers sat at a table. A single candle guttered in the draught. They were drinking tea they had boiled with a tommy cooker. "Poor old Jim," said one. "After eighteen months. He missed this." There was more talk in like vein. Then came three tiny raps at the window.

"Angel of Mons," said the man in the corner. "Come for his money."

Again the rapping, and a lad got up and looked. A face was at the window, pallid, worn, terrible, humanity just existing. On the head was a shiny cap with a tiny flag in it. "It's a civilian," said the lad. "He's got a barrow, a woman, two kids and a dog. He wants to know if he can go home."

"Where's his home?" asked the corporal.

"Petit Monde." "Petit Monde!" It was a rubble heap in No Man's Land.

"Tell him to go back where he's come from,"

"But he says he's been four years with Heinie, and the war's over. . . ."

Then the face stirred in a thin smile, and nodded.

"Blimey," said the corporal, "he's thanking us."

Twelve francs those boys in the cellar had, to spend in Mons next day, and they gave the wretch every cent, and the rest of the tea they had brewed. The woman drank it without comment. She had endured beyond the line of any emotion.

The boys returned to their table.

"It's goin' to be years before the war's over for some," said one.

"It aint ever goin' to be over for a lot of blokes," said another.

"Canada doesn't know what war means," said the third.

"Where'll we be ten years from now?" said the first.

He had been blown up by a shell at Vimy, and had continual headaches after he came home. Finally he got so he could not sleep. After three years he walked into a canal and got rid of the pain.

The second lad, he who talked with the refugee, had swallowed plenty of gas. He's got a regular soldiers' grave up in Ontario.

The third man was in the bread line in his home town last winter. His hair is gray. He enlisted at seventeen, and he is physically worn out today. He had thirty-two months in the trenches.

Of course he gets no pension. There wasn't enough evidence.

"The years pass, thy memory remains."

November 18th, 1933

THEY TELL the story of the "black sheep" in a First Division battalion who liked his rum in large issue, and who got properly "tanked" one morning at the front just as the brigadier came to visit the trenches. There was no deep dugout in which the inanimate one could be placed, and desperate wits evolved the idea of placing him on a stretcher and covering him over with a blanket.

This was hastily done, and the next moment the gilded and mighty one had arrived. He saw the stretcher, paused, and saluted.

"Greater love hath no man than..... " He repeated the full verse.

Then, from under the blanket, in muffled tones, was heard, "What in the..... is that..... old bird sayin'?"

We've had the 2nd C.M.R. version of the barrier, and now for the report of the 4th C.M.R.:

"On Dec. 3rd, a patrol discovered a German working party on the Wulverghem-Messines Road beyond the low ground in the rather wide No Man's Land on this sector. The next day it was discovered that a barrier had been erected across the road. The weather was unfavourable, it had been raining for several days, visibility was poor and the artillery was unsuccessful in an attempt to remove it. Consequently General Seeley came into the lines and asked for volunteers to raid the barrier. The raiding party was to get prisoners for identification purposes, if possible; find out the reasons for such a barrier; make a reconnaissance and return within the hour. Lieut. G.W. Rutter, a sergeant, a corporal and ten men of "C" Squadron volunteered. The party started about 10 P.M. and were supported by another party located in front of the trench, and also by one in the trenches under Capt. Donald McKay. The raid was to take place behind the screen of an artillery bombardment, but, unfortunately, this drew the enemy's fire in a counter-bombardment and put the opposing troops on the alert. Lieut. Rutter scattered his party, took one man and crossed the ground to the barrier, making a complete reconnaissance, although entirely exposed to the enemy by flares and rockets which lighted the whole ground. Due to the bombardment there were several casualties. Capt. McKay, Privates B. Tracey, and R. Sears were killed and four men wounded."

That was the attempt of the 4th C.M.R.

Their raids were usually successful. On March 30th, '17, Lieut. E.G. Richards led a battle patrol between Devon and Vernon craters into the enemy's line. The patrol, divided into two parties of three men each, one under Corpl. Martin, the other under Corpl. Dawson, crawled in the dark to the enemy's parapet. They saw three Germans whom they bombed and killed; in the next bay they killed two more. By this time the enemy was aroused and the raiders withdrew. Lieut. Richards was badly wounded. A short time before, he and Lieut. T. W. E. Dixon entered the German trenches in front of Ecurie and nailed up a sign : "Come over and we will treat you right."

At Passchendaele five men of the 4th C.M.R.'s who were recommended for the Military Medal received the Distinguished Conduct Medal. It reminds me of an officer who was twice recommended for the Victoria Cross, and received an Military Cross and second award bar, and of a non-com who was three times recommended for the D.C.M. and got the M.M. and two bars. Good luck to those C.M.R. boys. One thing is sure; they all earned them.

And speaking of medals reminds us of many arguments about which battalion won the most Victoria Crosses. That's a hard one, for immediately each unit claims the honors won by every man who at one time wore their badges. Thus, if a man served for a time with the 13th, went to the 24th and with them earned a V.C., the 13th at once advertise it as an honor of their battalion - while the 24th, of course, count it as their crowning glory, which is right. On that basis, one would never settle the disputes. As far as I can learn, however, the V.C.s won by members of units while with the unit, gives the proper rating thus:

- four - 16th;
- three - 7th, 8th, 13th;
- two - 2nd, 3rd, 10th, 14th, 20th, 22nd, 27th, Princess Patricia's Canadian Light Infantry, 49th, 5th C.M.R., 38th, and 78th;
-one - 1st, 4th, 5th, 18th, 24th, 29th, Royal Canadian Regiment, 42nd, 2nd C.M.R., 4th C.M.R., 43rd, 52nd, 58th, 46th, 47th, 50th, 75th, 87th, 102nd.

On March 4th, 1918, 8,403 women were employed in the Royal Flying Corps, including 2,969 clerks, 1,322 storemen, 899 sail-makers, 263 fitters, 153 riggers, 436 mechanical transport drivers and 680 cooks.

The Ghurkas were very expert with those crooked blades they carried, according to a story our sergeant used to tell. One night up at Neuve Chapelle a Ghurka crawled over in the dark until he was alongside the German sentry, and made a quick cut at him.

"Ah-ha", said Heinie, stepping back. "You missed me that time, you. . . . black man."

"That so," said the Ghurka. "You try shake your head."

Heinie shook his head-and it tipped off into the trench !

From 12th June, 1915, to 1st March, 1917, 160 officers with the Royal Flying Corps were killed by accident in England.

R.F.C., killed and missing on the Western Front:

1916

July -	75
August -	66
September -	105
October -	75
November -	59
December -	39

1917

January -	41	July -	168
February -	65	August -	183
March -	143	September -	214
April -	316	October -	198
May -	18	November -	193
June -	165	December -	81

1918

January -	96
February -	91
March -	245
April -	194
May -	240
June -	211
to July 21st -	200

When the "Van-doos" made their drive into Courcelette they captured two colonels. One was a Baron, a regimental commander, and he was a large and dignified man. He frowned on Colonel Tremblay, in command of the victorious Van-doos, took out a beautiful silver cigarette case, and removed a wonderful gold-tipped cigarette. It was a time when smokes were scarce, but he offered none to his captors and haughtily ignored them. The wounded were collected in the low ground of the village, but the shelling began to near them, and an N.C.O. took the German Red Cross flag that was on a building, went to a high point and waved it so that it could be seen. There were more German wounded than Canadian exposed, but the Baron saw that he and his men were not being watched closely and chose the moment to attempt an attack on their captors, whom they out-numbered.

The 22nd, however, was too quick for them. A number of the Germans were bayoneted in short order, or shot, and the rest "kameraded" a second time. The Baron had been promptly shot in the leg by a small runner, and, with the wound, all his dignity fled him. He begged for his life in a most grotesque posture, and his surrender was accepted. (There is a persistent cook-house rumour to the effect that the Baron was accidentally napooed on the way back. Does anybody know the truth?).

November 25th, 1933

PRIVATE SANDY McNickel got married while he was home on leave, and rejoiced considerably about it when he returned to the platoon, wondering what so-and-so would say when they heard about her.

"Forget it," growled Sergt. Taylor. "Your wife won't be noticed any more'n anybody else. She hasn't got a brass band with her, has she?"

"She has that," said Donal Dunwodies, bitter enemy of Sandy's. "She'll be carryin' it on her finger."

And when we got to Valenciennes old Tom Mell went with the corporal to look at the
Art Gallery which the Germans had robbed. There was, however, many paintings and
statues remaining, mostly of ladies in the nude. Old Tom regarded them intently for
quite a time, then turned to the corporal.
    "Well, if that's how they ought to be, Corp.," he remarked sadly, "they made a bit
of a mess of my old woman."

Do you know that a woman won the Victoria Cross? At least she was awarded a gold
replica of the real thing, for not until 1920 did women become eligible for the honor.
In 1869, Mrs. Webber Harris nursed the men of her husband's regiment, the 104th
Bengal Fusiliers, through a terrible epidemic of cholera, saving more than a score of
lives by her heroism and unselfish service. As the V.C. could not be awarded, the men
and officers had a gold replica of the medal made and presented it to her. It is now in
the Royal United Service Museum at Whitehall, London.

The Germans handed over to the Allies:

Aeroplanes in good condition	1,781
Aeroplanes in bad condition	932
Total	**2,713**

Distinguished Conduct Medals, Military Medals and Meritorious Service Medals
could be awarded without limit in France, Egypt, Salonica, Mesopotamia, Italy. 200
Distinguished Service Orders and 500 Military Crosses were permitted each month
in France. 25 D.S.O.s and 60 M.C.s per month to Egypt. 10 D.S.O.s and 20 M.C.s per
month to Salonica. 3 D.S.O.s and 6 M.C.s per month to East Africa. 20 D.S.O.s and
40 M.C.s per month to Mesopotamia. 6 D.S.O.s and 15 M.C.s per month to Italy. 2
M.C.s, 5 D.C.M.s and 10 M.M.s per month to Aden and adjacent territory.

During the war 12,000 acres were cultivated by the British Expeditionary Force on
the Salonica front. In Mesopotamia 750,000 acres were farmed by the B.E.F. and
civilians.

The soldier's ration in France was supposed to be - Meat, 1 lb.; bread, 1 lb.; bacon, 4
oz.; cheese, 2 oz., fresh or dried vegetables, 8 or 2 oz. 1/2 tea, oz. ; jam, 3 oz. ; but-

ter, 2 oz. ; sugar 3 oz. ; oatmeal, 2 oz.; salt, 1/4 oz.; milk (condensed),1 oz.; rice (issued as an extra), 1 oz.; pickles (thrice weekly),1 oz. The average "old sweat" who did his six "off" and six "on" along the crater line the winter of '16-'17 knows how faithfully this allowance was followed.

All returning prisoners of war were issued, on arrival, with 1 pint tea, 1/2lb. hot meat and potato pie and 3 oz. rock cake. All were issued with a "luxury parcel" consisting of 1 pipe, 1 oz. tobacco, 20 cigarettes, 1/4 lb. sweetened biscuits, 1 packet of chocolate or toffee. 162,793 prisoners received these treats.

There were 503 officers sentenced to be cashiered. 377 sentences were carried out, 88 sentences were commuted, 74 were commuted to dismissal,14 forfeited seniority, 10 were quashed, 23 were not confirmed, 5 were remitted.

There were 1,420 officers sentenced to be dismissed. 1,085 sentences were carried out, 278 were commuted, 17 were quashed, 36 were not confirmed, 4 were remitted.

There were 730 General Courts-Martials for the trials of soldiers in the United Kingdom, and 94 civilians. There were 137,683 District Courts-Martials for the trials of soldiers in the United Kingdom. There were 267 G.C.M.s for soldiers at the front, and 5,326 D.C.M.'s.

There was a total of 304,262 trials of soldiers at home and abroad during the war, and the crime most punished was the familiar A.W.L. (absent without leave), There were 88,188 such cases. Next in line were "miscellaneous military offences," not saluting properly, minus a belt, etc. Third was "drunkenness." Other crimes were "offence against an inhabitant," "mutiny," "theft," "resisting an escort," "self-inflicted wound," of which there were 3,904 cases, 12 of them officers, "desertion," "cowardice," "war treason," "false answer," "fraudulent enlistment," "neglect," etc.

The longest sentence given was "life," handed out in 143 cases. 461 were sentenced to "15 years," and 1,874 to "12 years." Of course the majority of those sentences were suspended after war. 9,468 sentences were "suspended" at the court proceedings. There were 8,806 Courts-Martial proceedings on Conscientious Objectors.

Remember Madame Tussaud's world-famous waxworks? It's more wonderful than ever since the fire, especially the "War" part. The Sultan of Zanzibar carne to London for a visit, and had his son with him. They went to the waxworks. They saw the Hall of Kings, where all the monarchs from William the Conqueror to Edward VII stand in gallant array, and they admired their armor very much. Then the Sultan went on to admire the group representing the present Royal Family, and all the while he kept talking to his son, telling him who the Royalty were, etc. At last they came to the "war" section, and stopped to gaze at the Naval Victoria Cross winner, Boy Cornwall.

"So young," murmured the Sultan. "Very young."

He saw other great leaders, generals with rows of bright ribbons and proper military jowls. Then he stopped.

The Sultan was gazing with wide, bright eyes at the immortal Old Bill, in his dirty khaki and tin hat, and walrus moustache. He had no eyes for generals or gleaming admirals.

Turning, he caught his son by the arm, and spoke impressively.

"This," he said with great dignity, "is the man who won the war."

Chapter 12: December 1933

December 2nd, 1933

"Said a tin-hatted gentleman, "Beer
    In this country's a great deal too dear;
        Till we all get it free
        This 'ere land won't be
    A plice fit for 'eroes, I fear.

"Sergt. McHubbard went down to his cupboard,
An issue to give his `interim,'
        But when he got there,
        His cupboard was bare,
    A batman 'ad been there before 'im."
                From *The Dragon.*

During the war discipline ruled supreme on every craft.

"Man overboard!" came the hoarse and fearful shout. Boats were lowered and a search made. Later the ship's company were lined up and a roll-call read; the mystery deepened, for no one was missing. At length an Able Bodied Seaman stepped forward.

"I think, sir," he said to the officer,"'as' ow I'm, the man. I went over, sir, but I managed to catch the anchor chain an' climbed in again."

"Then why on earth didn't you say so before?"

"Very sorry, sir, but I 'adn't time. I'm on the lifeboat crew, sir, an' I had to go wiv' 'em to look for the man overboard."

Can any Canadian battalion equal the decoration record of the "Fighting Thirteenth" Battalion of the Australian Imperial Force? Lieutenant-Colonel Murray, V.C., C.M.G., D.S.O. (and bar), D.C.M., Croix de Guerre; Maurice Buckley, Sergeant Gerald Sexton, V.C., D.C.M. Six D.S.O.s and a bar; 33 M.C's and a bar; 31 D.C.M.s; 188 M.M.s and 7 bars. Counting foreign decorations, the 13th were awarded 288 honors.

Edwin Pye, ex-5th Battalion, has a splendid article on the "Barrier," in the October number of the *Ypres* Times.

He describes a call on the owners of Petite Douve Farm by the Uhlans in '14, which resulted in nothing more than a bad scare. The farmer had grown grain and tobacco along the valley of the Douve for many years. British cavalry came next, and shells fell near, so the farmer moved back to Trois Rois, on the Neuve Eglise road, where the mother and older daughter made money catering to troops in reserve at Aldershot and Bulford camps.

In the summer of '15 the British feared that the Germans were mining from the Petite Douve Farm, and the farmer's wife was questioned about the cellars there, etc. Patrols were sent out and a constant watch was kept. He writes :

"During the occupancy of the Douve sector by Canadians the Germans, working from a ruined cottage east of the Messines road in No Man's Land, and screened by a tree which had been felled conveniently adjacent by our artillery, constructed a barricade across the road. The new work was discovered at noon of Dec. 3rd by the 2nd C.M.R. who, as soon as it was dusk, sent out a patrol which made a close inspection of the barricade and, after throwing several bombs, returned and made report.

The advanced position was 110 yards from our front line and about the same distance from the German trenches. It was strongly constructed, being bricked at the base and built up by sandbags. To permit such boldness with impunity was not to be tolerated, and orders were given for its immediate capture. But this was easier said than done.

Torrential rains had made a quagmire of the trenches, in which men wallowed up to their waists. Nepean Ave., the main Communication Trench, contained four feet of water, and the deepened ditch along the edge of the Messines road was equally impassable. Added to this, the Douve had risen and both flanks of the barrier rested on the flooded river. The attack was made on the morning of Dec. 4th, but proved abortive.

General Staffs worked overtime in calling for and working on reports. The advanced post, allowed to remain, would have menaced the lives of our patrols and working parties. Another attack was made by Strathcona's Horse on the night of 8-9 Dec. Twenty Germans swarmed out and showed open fight, and a sharp bombing action ensued, resulting in 11 casualties to the attacking party. Then the 5th Battalion volunteered to return to the trenches and make a determined effort to capture the stronghold. They had held that sector previously.

They moved in on Dec. 10th and scouts went out at once, but their presence was soon known to the German garrison when they stumbled upon a clever trip wire which exploded a series of bombs. An attack was carried out on the morning of the 15th. A 15-minute bombardment was put down in the afternoon, and at night on the 12th, 13th and 14th, and for five minutes only, from 4 A.M. of the 15th. An attacking force, three parties of 1 officer and 14 men each, were got ready. On the afternoon of the 13th the defenders of the barricade bolted overland during the bombardment, and six were shot, five by Sergeant J.S. McGlashen (later Major, M.C., D.C.M.), while the remainder scuttled back to cover. On the night of the 14th the 3rd Battery, Canadian Field Artillery, placed an 18-pounder in the front line opposite the barrier. The gun was towed up the Messines road to Chateau de la Hutte by an armored car of "A" Battery, 1st Canadian Motor Machine Gun Brigade, then man-handled to position. Two and a half feet of parapet were hauled down to make an opening. The gun fired 3 rounds of High Explosive and 22 rounds of shrapnel at point-blank range, then something happened to its mechanism, but its work had been accomplished. The attackers met no opposition. There were only two living men in the debris. Four mangled forms were removed, then the position was mined against further occupation and the raiders withdrew, bringing in seven rifles and a bag of bombs as souvenirs. The prisoners were Bernhard Elesse and Paul Rosner, 3rd Battalion,11th Reserve Infantry, Regiment, 117th Division, both volunteers for duty at the barricade.

The armored car was run to the gun to make a quick get-away. But within 200 yards of the front trench it mired. Another car came-and went through a plank bridge. Car No.1 was righted and pulled out, with the gun. It then hauled out car No.2. Driver Frank Waghorn (later Lieut., M.C., D.C.M.), was at the wheel. So ran the story; I have condensed it from Pye's account.

Paddy Flynn could never figure where the French got red oil from for those little signal lamps they had at the stations.

December 9th, 1933

IN A little parlor in Sussex the chief ornament on the wall is a framed "Crown and Anchor" cloth. It has an interesting history. Just before the Somme battle in the village back of the lines a crowd was gathered in a corner billet.

"Crahn an' Anchor. Wot abaht a little more on the ol' mud'ook? Nah, then, 'oo syes a bit more on the Club? Wot abaht the ol' shovel? If yer don't speculate yer can't accumulate. Oo'll 'ave a wyber on the king's 'at? Yer put dahn centimes an' yer pick up francs."

It was a high game that night, for on the morrow. . . . Pte. Sydney Perkins made almost four hundred French francs, and tucked it away carefully in a big roll inside his tunic.

Came the attack next morning. The attackers reached the first trench in front of Mametz, then were shelled, and one explosion blew in the captured trench, burying Perkins.

"Come along," said the sergeant. "They're all dead under a 'eap like that."

But three men lagged behind. They had seen the roll that Perkins carried, and they began to dig for it. Finally they reached him, and he was still alive. A broken timber had been standing in such a way that it provided an air shaft. He was wounded, and had an arm broken, but Perkins lived. And he GAVE HIS RESCUERS HIS ROLL.

Back home, he had his "Crahn and Anchor" framed, for if he hadn't played it he'd still be under the piled earth.

Paddy Flynn went on parade one morning with a "kitchen mark" of black across the arm of his tunic. He discovered it at the last moment, when there was no time to remove it. Along came the officer.

"And who," he demanded with heavy sarcasm,"are you in mourning for?"

"For yirsilf, sir," came Paddy's surprising answer. "I dreamt last night that ye were killed badly, and it was so rale that I put on me black before I was thinkin'."

He spoke so earnestly that the officer paled and said no more to him.

Twelve years after the war the British House of Commons, on a free vote, carried by 219 votes to 135, an amendment to the annual Army Bill abolishing the death penalty for desertion. The chief speaker said that one of the limits beyond which they might not go, even for the sake of military necessity, was to have a man shot in cold blood by his fellow-countrymen because his nerves had failed to stand the strain of modern warfare. He said the death penalty was not applied to Australian troops during the war.

"If it can be demonstrated that the Australians could fight as gallantly as they did without the death penalty, then it is a libel on the courage of other British troops to say they won't fight without it," he declared.

As with so many other things, what a pity to high Heaven these men had not made such decisions before-not after-the war. They cannot bring the dead to life. And, I'd like to say, in passing, two Australians were put to the wall during the war, and there were certain crimes for which a member of the A.I.F. could be given the extreme penalty.

Duplicate war medals can be obtained from the War Office, on payment, in cases where it can be proved that the lost medals are irrecoverable. Upon application a form is available which is filled in with all particulars and sworn before a magistrate. It must be clearly understood, however, that lost medals cannot be replaced if the recipient is deceased.

There are 71,620 unclaimed medals of the Australians awaiting owners, among them a Distiguished Service Order and Medaille de Sauvetage, and a Croix de Guerre.

When Lieut Dander went on leave he got married. He went up to Edinburgh on his honeymoon, and at the hotel tipped the maid a half-crown, asking her, after she had seen the confetti they shed in their room, not to give away the secret that they were newly married.

But a gossipy old girl was waiting in the corridor. "Newly married couple in there, eh " she questioned.

"No," said ,the maid, loyal to the half-crown, "they're just friends."

Infractions of the Armistice Clauses

"Delivery of War Material." On Dec. 9th the following were delivered or abandoned: 1,635 heavy guns instead of 2,500 which should have been delivered on Dec. lst. 2,000 Minenwerfer instead of 3,000 per Armistice terms. 18,000 machine guns instead of 25,000. 730 fighting and bombing planes instead of 1,700. 1,999 were abandoned, but these include 200 observation planes; and 1,000 are in bad condition, 600 absolutely unfit for use.

"Safeguarding of Inhabitants and Property." At Charleroi explosions were instigated by the Germans after Nov. 11th. There were outrages against persons and property at Maastricht. Prisoners were set free en masse and sent across the Allied lines without means of obtaining shelter or food-thus rendering it most difficult for the Allies to receive them. A number of these died from exhaustion. In spite of protests by French and British Governments this inhuman procedure continued. On 27th November 16 prisoners (9 French, 3 English, 2 Italians, 2 Russians) were killed at Langensalza Camp, and 24 were wounded. In this camp 1,000 prisoners were in the hospital without medicaments or medical care.

The German reply to this was that they had appointed a Commission with full power to bring the culprits to justice, and that many sick and wounded Germans who had been left behind were very badly treated. Minor rebellions and political disturbances had lessened all discipline until it was difficult to maintain any order or fulfil obligations.

A new man who joined us at Lozinghem was a graduate of McGill, and tried to poke fun at Sergeant Taylor's use of language. Taylor called him "'Arrison."

"My name's not 'Arrison," said the newcomer. Taylor flared. "If an haitch, a hay, two hars, a hi a hes, a ho and a hen, don't spell 'Arrison, wot does?"

December 16th, 1933

WHEN THE war was over our Major Grimm hurried back to Canada to resume his business in Montreal, and he booked hurriedly on a liner leaving Liverpool. Space was limited, and the purser hastily assigned him to a stateroom to be shared with another officer, Major H. Wallow. A few hours later Grimm hunted up the skipper, wildly indignant.

"This is no kind of a joke," he spluttered. "I can't and won't stay in that room with Major Wallow."

"What's wrong?" queried the harassed skipper. "We're crowded, and officers simply have to share rooms."

"But this here's a Salvation Army officer," yelled Grimm, "and the Major's other name is `Henrietta' "

Paddy had been strong for his beer, and our new officer was a temperance advocate. He tried to show Paddy the error of his ways when we were passing the transport lines at Houdain.

"Take a donkey," he said, "and lead him up to a pail of water and a pail of beer. Which will he drink?"

"The water," said Paddy.

"Right," said the officer heartily, "and why?"

"Because, sir, said Paddy, "the poor baist's an ass."

Sixty-eight officers were promoted from the ranks of the Sixteenth Australian Battalion. Can any Canadian battalion equal that record?

Ten years after the war 22,000 Australian veterans had died.

The total number of British (only) wounded was 1,527,711.

United States Army in France, 1918:

	Ration strength	Combatant strength	Rifle strength
11th March	245,000	123,000	49,000
1st April	319,000	214,000	51,000
25th Sept.	1,641,000	1,195,000	341,000
11th Nov.	1,924,000	1,160,000	322,000

Comparisons of capture between 18th July and 11th November:

	Prisoners	Guns
British Armies	200,000	2,540
French Armies	135,720	1,880
American Armies	43,300	1,421
Belgian Armies	14,500	474

The Poisoned Arrows from the Air

Generals Ludendorff and Hindenburg told Germany after the war that the morale of the German Army had largely been destroyed by the "poisoned arrows from the air." This was the British and Allied propaganda which was showered over their lines and in their billeting villages. These were first scattered by our airmen, then distributed by means of hydrogen balloons, sent over when the wind was favourable. The

Courier de l'Air was a sprightly little paper. Its object was to give the inhabitants of occupied territories in France and Belgium accurate news of the progress of the war-from the Allied viewpoint. The average number distributed was 5,000 per week.

The front page contained the latest news from the battle lines. The back page was filled with extracts, translated into French, from papers of the Allied countries, and especially from German papers, suppressed by the Government when they reflected adversely upon the conduct of the war, or upon the frightful conditions existing in Germany from April '17, when the Courier started until the finish. Extracts were used from British, Belgian, Italian, Spanish, French and Dutch papers, as well as from ten German ones. One choice bit was copied from the German *Vienna Witzblatt*, throwing lurid light upon the agonies of the civilian population. It was a dialogue between two women in a tramcar. Said the first:

"I had a wonderful dream last night-I dreamt that the war was over."

The other: "What did you have to eat?"

"I don't know."

"What a stupid dream."

The German High Command hated the *Courier*. Major von Blucher, the Commandant at Ghent, threatened the inhabitants with a fine of five hundred dollars or a year's imprisonment, or both, if they failed to hand over immediately, and *unread*, any copy of the paper that fell from the air. For the first copy brought in the "Kommandantur" paid ten francs-for every subsequent one 25 centimes (in German paper).

The first copy was immediately translated into German and sent to every Kommandantur in the occupied territory, and distributed to spies who circulated among the people. If one of them heard a bit of news that obviously came from the sheet he was arrested at once and made to tell where he heard it; his informant was next arrested, and so on, until the holder of the paper was found and punished.

Millions of leaflets in German were written by scholarly prisoners of war, who regarded their capture as an emancipation from the horrors of hell, and implored their fellow countrymen to realize that they could never win, and extolled the social charm and abundant food which were the lot of German prisoners in British camps. One curious thing was learned early-the German soldiers and civilians did not wish any abuse of the Emperor. They liked best the reprints from their own Social-Democrat papers, which were suppressed the moment they appeared.

Propaganda sheets were threaded on silk paper fasteners a dozen at a time, and these were in turn threaded through strips of yellow tinder about a yard long, and "fortified" by a copper wire running through them. These were called "releases," and were sent over in vast quantities together with an ample supply of paper balloons. Up to March '18 these were loosed by our airmen. Then the Germans imprisoned any airmen so caught, and two of the aviators were sentenced to ten years' penal servitude. This was averted by threatened reprisals, but balloons were then used altogether. One letter written by a prisoner to his wife dwelt so strongly on his splendid food, etc., that it was copied with facsimile so clever that it was difficult to tell which was the original. The copies were broadcast. Then came his wife's reply : "I was delighted to get your letter, but now I fear it is not genuine, for I have received 27 copies of it." People had found them and, imagining they were lost, posted them to her.

At Bourecq Paddy was busy with a pencil and Y.M.C.A. paper. "I'm writin' in for this special impassionate leave," he said. "I want six weeks in Canada. Who'll I address it to?"

"Santa Claus," snorted Sergt. Taylor.

December 23rd, 1933

IT WAS rumored around billets that the battalion as a whole was not in love with the spit-and-polish unit known as the "Royal Canadian Regiment." The soldiers themselves were good fellows and we sympathized with them, but...those "Shino Kings!"

Then the story got around that an officer of the Royals died and was to be given a proper burial, but their padre was on leave. They applied to our wearer of the cloth, and he decided to phone to the O.C. for instructions. The reply sizzled over the wires.

"Bury all R.C.R.s possible."

Cockney Joe was going home on leave when he got to talking with a prim old lady in the railway carriage.

"We've come from Wipers-" Joe began.

"Ypres," corrected the old lady.

..I said as 'ow we've come from Wipers-"

"Ypres," said the old lady.

Joe glanced at her sharply and tried once more.

"We've moved from Wipers-"

"Ypres."

"Lor, missus," said Joe, "you ain't 'arf got hiecups."

December 25th, 1914 by E.P.L., in The Ypres Times.

"The most wonderful and, perhaps, weird Christmas ever spent. Picture opposing lines of trenches, from 100 yards apart in one place to 400 yards in another, and you have the wet and muddy ditch comprising the front line before Wez Macquart. All the late afternoon the desultory sniping and usual shelling have gone on, but at "stand-to" an astonishing thing happened. Several men appeared behind the German lines carrying lanterns. Fire was immediately opened on them, which evoked cries of "Don't shoot," in English. Suspecting some new ruse, we held our fire, but kept on the "qui vive" and the Jerries disappeared into their trench. Suddenly lights began to appear all along the whole Boche parapet until his front line was illuminated for a mile or more, and a voice called across in good English, inviting one man to meet the owner halfway across No Man's Land, and he would exchange a bottle of wine and a box of cigars for a cake.

A volunteer was quickly found and it was most weird to watch the two pinpoints of light (each carried a flash-lamp) go toward each other. They met, and our man found, not one, but three Jerries. However, the exchange was duly made, and by now we were all sitting on our parapet, and an eerie silence seemed to pervade the atmosphere, while behind, in the villages, huge bonfires were being made by celebrating troops. The guns were silent. The Spirit of Christmas was abroad. Peace on earth, good-will toward men. Meanwhile an officer on our right had gone across under a flag of truce and arranged an armistice for the morrow. They were a Saxon "mob" opposite, and their commander concluded by saying : "A truce until midnight tomorrow, when I will fire my automatic and the war will continue." As the news spread, the boys were out in front eager to stretch their legs after having been up to their knees in water. One of our platoons started up a carol and at the end there was applause from the other side. Then Jerry sang to us and the, quaintest concert was carried out, each side rendering a carol or a song, and evoking applause from the other. An imaginary line was drawn across No Man's Land, and here- they met the Jerries and exchanged bully beef galore for chocolate, wine, cigars and other luxuries. Next morning, Christmas, broke fine and frosty, and after "stand-to" the same procedure was carried out. It was a real treat to get up on top without having a bullet zip by one's ear. Some lads from the neighboring battalion were parading up and down a road behind our line, attired, one in a frock coat and silk hat, another in female dress, complete with picture hat and sunshade, and a third on a ramshackle bicycle. We were relieved that same night, after a very pleasant day, and marched back to Houplines. And were the Brass Hats wild. After they had recovered from their feasting in their cushy chateaus, they sent out drastic orders that the soldiers were hereafter to kill each other at every chance, and never to be friendly again. Read what Sir Philip Gibbs had to say about the winter of ' 15.

"When the wind dropped at dusk or dawn a whitish fog crept out of the ground, so that the rifles were clammy to the touch and a blanket of moisture settled on every stick in the dugouts.

Our men were never dry. They were wet in their trenches and in their shelters. They slept in soaking clothes with boots full of water, and they drank rain with their tea, and ate mud with their bully. . . .

On the other side of the wire the Germans were more miserable, because they lacked the English sense of humor, "How deep is it with you?" they shouted.

"Up to our bloomin' knees," said a corporal.

"So. You are lucky. We are up to our belts in it."

The Germans crawled on their slimy parapets and shouted, "Don't shoot-don't shoot."

Our men didn't shoot. They, too, sat on their parapets and dried their legs-until those incidents were reported back to G.H.Q- where good. fires were burning under dry roofs-and stringent orders came against "fraternization." Every German who showed himself was to be shot. . . . the dignity of G.H.Q. would not be enraged by the thought of such indecent spectacles as British and Germans refusing to kill each other on sight.

Above a German trench appeared a plank on which, in big letters, was scrawled these words: "The English are fools."

It was smashed to splinters by rifle fire. Another plank appeared : "The French are fools."

It, too, was splintered. A third plank went up. "We are all fools. Let's all go home."

But neither side was prepared to go "home" first. Loyalty spells words of old tradition, all the moral and spiritual propaganda handed out by pastors, newspapers, generals, old men at home, exalted women, female furies, a deep and simple love for England and Germany. . . prevented men from breaking the net of fate in which they were entangled and revolting against that mutual, unceasing massacre. . . ."

From "A Winter of Discontent."

December 30th, 1933

ONE OF the new draft announced that he had been a barber in civil life, and set up shop at Lozinghem the morning after pay parade. Paddy Flynn decided that he would have the luxury of getting shaved without borrowing soap, warm water, a mirror and razor, his usual procedure. The new man operated with more zeal than skill and snagged his weapon several times in the deep furrows about Paddy's mouthpiece. At last he was finished, and Paddy sat up and asked for the lad's waterbottle.

"You're not feelin' faint, are you?" asked the `barber' anxiously. "I kinda nicked you there at the corners of your mouth but. . . ."

"I just wan to see," said Paddy, before gettin a swig, "whether or not me mouth will hold water."

We are the Missing Generation,

(by Gerald Bullett, in the London Evening News.)

"They are inconspicuous; and they have little or nothing to say about it themselves. But in certain significant respects they are so different from the younger and older men as to constitute a separate species. It is difficult indeed to put one's finger on the difference, but every sensitive person must at one time or another have been aware of it. They are now, most of them, in the late thirties or early forties, and you may encounter them in the Savoy Theatre watching a play which, though all admire, they alone can fully understand ("Journey's End").

Intently, without visible emotion, they stare at that scene in the dugout. A wonderful and terrible scene that tightens the nerves and sets the heart jumping. But these men make no fuss. They spent four years learning not to make a fuss, and the habit persists. What their feelings are you are welcome to imagine if you can; it is more than they will ever tell you.

It is not that they refuse to talk about the war. Among themselves they do sometimes. But they do not, because they cannot, even among themselves, tell the whole truth about it. The unspeakable cannot be spoken. They know what they know; they know it intimately; and that intimate knowledge is a scar on the soul. When you meet one of them and fall into conversation with him you become gradually aware of this something different that distinguishes him and his kind. It may be manifested in some nervous little trick, some strangeness in manner, some reserve that seems abnormal and hints at a `complex.' And he may or not be suffering still from the effects of mutilation, shell-shock, gassing.

But both the difference and its causes are more subtle than that. For four years these men, against their decent instincts, were taught to hold life cheap, and having yielded themselves body and brain to the war machine, were forced to take part in a monstrous crime against their own humanity.

A while ago a retired hangman tried to kill himself because only so could he forget his trade. I think some ex-soldiers feel like that. What they suffered no man can tell. They saw their comrades slaughtered. Death, in all its grotesque shapes, was their daily companion; and to kill was a duty imposed upon them by the terms of their nightmare.

There was no hatred in them. They left hating to the people at home-to hysterical women, men above the military age. They gave without stint and fought without malice; and now, more English than England herself, they are yet foreigners in their own country. The men who were old when they were young have learnt nothing, and a new generation has grown up to whom the war is no more than a remote historical event. The old are as ready as ever to fight with their mouths and shed tears in tribute to "the brave lads" who fall in a different kind of fighting; the young have better things to do. This is true of England, France and Germany. In America you do not notice the "missing generation"; the war has left no mark.

But of Britons the war destroyed a whole generation. Our ex-soldiers belong neither here nor there. A chasm divides them from the youngsters; and the chasm that always did divide them from the older folk has never been bridged. They are an inconvenient survival; or so they themselves secretly feel. They are the lonely ghosts of a vanished generation.

These men have not forgotten the war. They wouldn't if they could. When the enemy came and bombed from the air there was more indignation over one wounded civilian than over ninety and nine soldiers slaughtered in France. They were "innocent civilians." As though soldiers were to have a monopoly of the privilege of dying "for King and Country." In the next war there will be no respecter of persons. Patriotic young women and well-fed politicians will be no more immune from poison gas than the soldiers themselves. And if that fact can be driven home to the minds of warmongers, mercenary or romantic, there will be no next war.

The next War. After the Armistice we believed another war was "unthinkable." We know better now. We know that as surely as some of us are working for peace, so others are working against it. We hear again the old dreary argument, "it's only human nature to want a scrap now and then;" and I wish heartily that those who feel that need would march to Salisbury Plain and perforate each other with machine guns until they have had their fill.

We cannot learn from another's experience until we have made it imaginatively our own; that is why "Journey's End," stark and real and unsentimental, will do more for the cause of peace than any pious propaganda. And when the next war threatens, these men of the Missing Generation, no matter on which side they fought, can be depended upon to set their faces stubbornly against it. They will believe no promises, accept no excuses, listen to no arguments. They have seen war, and seen through it. For that reason, if for no other, they are worth cherishing."

And now, goodbye 1933. Greetings 1934. May it prove a better time. But it is men, not the time, or materials, that have put this old world in its muddle. Simply the minds and hearts of men. And had they one-half the fellowship of the trenches in their souls there would be no more wars, no preparing for them, and a prosperity beyond our dreams. The "spirit of the trenches" was a priceless potion.

Up at Loos a company went into action and was badly cut to pieces. When the remnant got back to their trench one boy, Jimmy, discovered that his pal was missing. He asked his officer if he might go back and look for him.

Reluctantly, the officer yielded. "But it isn't worth it, Jimmy," he said.

At long last Jimmy crawled back again, terribly and mortally wounded, and smiled up at the officer.

"It was worth it, sir," he said, "for when I reached him Bill said `I knew you would come.' "

That's friendship.

To all readers of this column I wish a most Happy and Glorious New Year.

Remember how the Second Division were blamed for looting in the spring of 1918. Kim Beattie has cleared it all up in his *History of the 15th Battalion.* And Douglas Oliver, who was an officer in the 18th Battalion, writes feelingly in the *Toronto Globe:* "For fourteen years this Division (Second) has rankled under the libel that its almost uninterrupted four-month period of raiding and dirty line-holding below Arras - at a time, too, when the other three divisions were resting in back country-was for "punishment" imposed upon it for looting the old city in the March swingdown from Vimy front. The libel may have originated as some idle cookhouse gossip, but over the years it has become so garbled, so grown and so galling as to drive many a temperamental veteran into fits of exasperation and expostulation.

What matter if Sir Douglas Haig had explained why the 2nd was kept in the line without relief ; that he wanted as many fully rested Canadian divisions for the subsequent Amiens show as he could muster? What matter if Sir Arthur Currie also offered his share of clarifying statements? Despite all contradiction and denials the slander stuck, and to mention "looting" to any member of the old "blue-patched" Burstall bunch has been just equal to inviting a good swift poke to the jaw.

At the time it happened the Second knew quite well it should not and could not be held accountable, because it never was billetted in Arras. But to fasten the blame where it belonged was more than it could manage-more, even, it appeared, than the Staff was inclined to tackle. Some valiant hearts did suggest that the 1st Division troops might have "mopped up" the town, but 1st Division troops kept their mouths shut, and any admissions they may have made were confined to their own family circle. Nothing got out for publication, that's sure. And so the slander stuck-right down to this moment when Mr. Beattie arrives on the scene with a splendid new story of the 15th Battalion and furnishes us with a first-hand and authentic glimpse of what was what and who was who in the Arras incident.

'The Highlanders,' he writes 'were the first troops to be warned of changed orders, as they had not reached as far south as many other units. So it was a footsore and still sleepy battalion (15th Battalion, 1st Division) that fell in and moved off at 4.15 A.M. to march up the sun as they swung towards Arras, which they reached at 7.30 A.M. on March 29, and immediately established a support position behind the 15th Battalion in the cellars of the Grande Place.

The air of uncertainty and doubt everywhere made the march unusual. A few miles from Arras and well behind the city, British Tommies were come on in a trench with their bayonets fixed and without knowing whether or not any one was between them and the front line.

When the battalion entered Arras their feet echoed hollowly on the cobbles down the empty streets of a deserted city. The inhabitants had fled and, with the exception of one military policeman, there was not one to greet them. All ranks were Confined to Barracks in the city, but that did not prevent the men from taking part in the 'Battle of Arras,' an infamous or famous action, according to whether it is the High Command's or the soldiers' point of view. The civilians had left in such haste that stores were not locked, neither were the champagne cellars, under the very floors on which they slept.

What wonder, then, that corks were popping? And how they popped ! Rumor said that some enterprising chefs poached eggs in the vintage of '79."

And so you know, at last, the truth about the "looting."

One man was killed every three minutes of the entire four years of war.

The 17th century caves under Arras were in hard chalk from 20 to 60 feet below the surface. The New Zealand Tunnelling Company drove tunnels 6 ft. 6 in. high by 4 ft. wide for a distance of three miles, and by these undergrounds troops could reach the front line. These were lighted by electricity.

Cave	Accommodation	Entrances	Description
Nelson	1,200	3	Power House
Wellington	1,500	7	Bad High roof
Blenheim	750	2	Discovered late
Auckland	300	4	Moderate roof
New Plymouth	500	3	Mostly passage
Russell	50	1	Small
Christchurch	4,075	10	40% floor
Dunedin	590	5	Bad roof
Bluff	460	4	Best roof
St Sauveur	2,000	13	Very low, bad roof

In *Military Mining Work of Royal Engineers*, '14-'18, the comment regarding Vimy is as follows: "Working of enemy on Vimy great in extent, but execution and lay-out poor, and costly in labor. Shallow and deep systems on the same level as ours. Considerable amount of good plant was found, but on the whole the work was decidedly inferior to that in the Somme area. The most striking thing was the visibility of our own spoil dumps, especially from subways. The whole position was overlooked from the German craters and the spoil stood out like monuments.

The work on Vimy was by four and a half companies. 8 mines were placed under the Boche but only 2 were used; the work on some were finished in October.

Thirteen subways were made, averaging _ mile in length, the shortest being 290 yards, the longest 1,880 yards. These were 6 feet 6 inches high, 3 feet wide, with 20 feet of head cover, lit by electricity, with a plant in each subway. All T.M. stores, and bomb stores, water tanks, dressing stations, signal offices, Brigade and Batt. Headquarters were installed. There were many exits. Maps were hung on boards as directions. Tramways were laid to bring in the stores, signal cables laid and water mains. Ventilation was good.

The subways were: Grange, Lichfield, and Goodman, worked by 172nd Company, Royal Engineers.

Cobourg, Souchez and Gobron, worked by 176th Coy., R.E.

Vincent, Cavalier, Valley, Tottenham and Blue Bull, worked by the 182nd Coy.

Douai, Bentata and Zivy, worked by the 185th Coy. Other Coys. were the 175th, 181st, 255th, and 258th British, and an Australian Coy., who looked after the electricity. A total of 6-1/4 miles of tunnel was completed."

Not many know that the owner of La Folie Farm buried 100,000 francs in his garden when the Germans were coming in 1914, and that some one found the money. For two years after the war the owner circulated inquiries in Canada, as Canadians were the probable finders.

That the New Zealanders found a large sum of money at Souchez. That one of the French spies working back of the German lines, who knew no Englishman, became dubious of his working arrangements, and was convinced of their sincerity by a unique method. He was asked what would make him believe he was actually in touch with the British Spy System, and said that if a certain munitions dump at a location he would give in Lille were shelled heavily at a time he would give, he would believe. The location was given, and the dump was shelled at once, though the British had not wanted to do so at that time; but they won his loyalty in the doing.

That a land machine was invented by a British marine officer and built in La Douve Valley, a huge monster that was to fill in all craters and trenches, levelling the battle fields. It weighed 28 tons and was to be driven by six large motors but failed to move from where it was constructed.

That the Germans had such good listening apparatus at Vimy in 1916 that they knew every move being made in the British lines. They have on their records all the telephone conversations between the Town Major of Villers au Bois and commanders of units in the front line, and so knew when each relief was made.

That 19,000 soldiers had their faces rebuilt by clever operations.

That one soldier has as many as 44 surgical operations.

That there are at least 160 deserters still in France who have never written home, know not who of their family is living, and have not seen a comrade of their old unit- and that the majority of them have remained single and dream continually of the day they dare go back. No pardon for them has ever been announced, and on the books they are listed as deserters.

That 38,630 all ranks were listed as "deserters" during the war.

That 502 Victoria Crosses were won in France and Belgium during the war, and Canadians, consisting of just one-sixteenth part of the B.E.F., won 53 of them.

That Bandsman "Paddy" Smith of the 27th Battalion went over the top on the 9th of April, at Vimy, playing the regimental march on his piccolo. He was killed shortly after reaching the objective.

That 80 per cent of the "mental cases" resulting from the war are from the unskilled laboring class.

That there will be no lice in the next war. A preparation like Zambuk has been invented as a cure for them.

That during the attack on Cambrai in 1917 an Eskimo of the Newfoundland Regiment met a German officer halfway across a footbridge over the canal and was seized by him. They struggled tremendously, and at the finish the Eskimo *bit the ear off* the German just before they both fell into the water and were drowned, still locked in combat.

That in the Hulluch area a continuous line of tunnels extended for four miles.

That Sniper Norwest, M.M., of the 50th Batalion., on April 28th, 1918, sniped his hundredth German.

That in German records it is found that the raid of March lst, 1917, was not so one-sided, as three dugouts of the 11th Bavarian Regt. were packed full, and every man perished when the raiders threw down Stokes shells.

That back in 1843 the British Army were issued the sawtooth bayonet.

COOKHOUSE RUMORS

Remember the story that went around about the riot at Etaples? The most persistent one was that a boxing match had taken place between an Military Police sergeant and a private of a Scots Battalion and that the private won. This enraged the Red Cap so that he picked a quarrel with the private afterward, got the worst of blows which followed and ended by shooting his rival with a revolver. This set the camp ablaze, and they rushed toward Paris Plage. Officers had been stationed at the bridge, but they were pushed aside, and the men went on, caught a bunch of the Red Caps and lynched them. The Town Major of Etaples came to the rescue, and was thrown in the mud, then into the harbour, but he only got wet; they didn't hurt him. Most of this work was done by Scots, with Aussies and Canadians ready to lend a hand. So ran the rumor.

Another cookhouse rumor was the one about the Ninth Brigade. Orders came that they were to march to the Rhine in full pack, and the men informed their non-coms and officers that if they had to walk all the way while the officers rode horses, their packs would certainly be taken on lorries or transport. It was said that even the Brigadier was interviewed. Then other 3rd Division men refused to go out on eight-hour drills and shine parades. The outcome was that orders arrived for the 3rd to stay in Belgium, and the fool parades were called off and more sensible ones substituted.

Canadian Casualties by Month

Year - 1915-	Officers	Other Ranks
January	4	27
February	5	130
March	21	434
April	198	3,958
May	142	3,148
June	49	1,019
July	18	292
August	11	254
September	12	322
October	37	986
November	37	810
December	36	202
- 1916 -		
January	34	602
February	22	549
March	46	1,073

	Officers	Other Ranks
April	157	3,718
May	101	2,495
June	484	10,021
July-	127	2,202
August	101	1,913
September	644	14,706
October	352	7,508
November	191	3,305
December	42	969
- 1917 -		
January	48	1,363
February	56	1,523
March	129	2,433
April	663	13,388
May	275	6,846
June	175	4,457
July	114	3,266
August	375	10,268
September	95	2,352
October	341	7,606
November	366	9,225
December	42	681
- 1918 -		
January	42	700
February	48	917
March	110	2,639
April	192	3,491
May	69	1,259
June	44	1,104
July	44	1,468
August	1,046	24,425
September	860	16,090
October	87	18,172
November	87	1,656

Sanctuary Wood, Ploegsteert Wood, and Polygon Wood are reported as "oak, larch, ash, beech, with undergrowth of hazel, alder, birch and maple." Langemark had 7,438 inhabitants before the war; Zonnebeke and Wytschaete, 3,500; Neuve Eglise, 2,311; Zillebeke, 2,081.

German stick bombs were manufactured almost entirely by their toy industry, and artillery fuses by the watch and clock makers.

There were in the United Kingdom 25,704 workers whose cards were 'starred', that is, they could not be taken from their trades to become soldiers.

The word "Artois," used so often in writing of France, is really obsolete. The Province of Artois was divided and made into the Departments of the Somme and Pas de Calais. There is no Artois.

In 1915 Sir Douglas Haig had a "dummy" headquarters, marked with his flag at Bethune, and German spies were completely deceived for more than two weeks.

Zillebeke Lake was "dug" as a reserve supply of water for the moat about Ypres.

And now for information about the gas attack of April 22, 1915. On the 14th the enemy fired a mine at St. Eloi and began a methodical bombardment, which roused some alarm. Next day the Second Army forwarded to General Headquarters the following report, brought by its liason officer with General Putz:

"A reliable agent of the Detachment of the French Army in Belgium reports that an attack on the Ypres Salient has been arranged for night 15-l6th April. (This was correct, but the wind was not favourable for gas.). A prisoner of the 234th Regiment XXVI Corps, taken on April 14th near Langemarck, reports that an attack had been prepared for noon 13th. Reserves have been brought up and passages have been prepared across old trenches existing in the rear of the present German trenches to facilitate bringing forward artillery.

The Germans intend making use of tubes with asphyxiating gas, placed in batteries of 20 tubes for every forty metres along the front of the XXVI Corps. (This planned line was wholly opposite the French). This prisoner had in his possession a small sack filled with a kind of gauze or cotton waste (cotton waste in a gauze bag) which would be dipped in some solution to counteract the effect of gas.

The German morale is said to have much improved lately, owing to the men having been told that there is not much in front of them.

It is possible that the attack may be postponed, if the wind is not favourable, so as to ensure that the gases blow over our trenches."

In sending this information, however, General Putz told the liaison officer that he did not believe it; for the prisoner, on further examination; exhibited such a knowledge of the German defences that he came to the conclusion that the fellow had been primed and sent over with the intention to deceive. On the following day, however,

No. 6 Squadron of the Royal Flying Corps was ordered to observe the German lines in the area mentioned for the express purpose of verifying the presence of any unusual apparatus. The airmen made reconnaissance on that date and on the following days without seeing anything unusual.

On the 16th further information came from Belgian sources to the effect that "the Germans have manufactured in Ghent 20,000 mouth protectors of tulle, which the men will carry in a waterproof bag 10 cm. by 17.5 cm. These mouth protectors, when soaked with a suitable liquid, serve to protect the men against the effects of asphyxiating gas."

That the prisoner's story was not the first warning the Staffs had. The following was in the Bulletin of the French Tenth Army of the 30th of March, 1915.

"According to prisoners of the XV Corps there is a large supply along the whole front in the neighbourhood of Zillebeke of iron cylinders 1.4 metres long, which are stored a little in the rear of the trenches in bomb-proof shelters, or even buried. They contain a gas which is to render the enemy unconscious or asphyxiate him. It has not yet been made use of, but the pioneers have received instructions regarding its use; the cylinder is laid on the ground pointing toward the enemy and is opened by withdrawing the cap; the gas is forced out by its own pressure, and remains near the surface of the ground; in order that the operation may be without danger for the operator a favourable wind is necessary. The pioneer detailed to open the cylinder has a special apparatus attached to his head; all the men are supplied with a cloth pad to be placed over the nostrils; the inventor has been promoted lieutenant."

But no action was ever taken by the British or French to prepare for a gas attack, or, for that matter, any form of attack.

Of the small villages near Ypres; Boesinghe had 2,263 inhabitants, St. Jean 851. Brielen 773.

German records state that the digging in of their gas cylinders was completed by Feb. 14th, and that by March 10th the entire front was so prepared, and they originally intended to launch the attack at Zillebeke; that shells damaged the cylinders several times and they had casualties in their own trenches; that when the British mined and captured Hill 60 on April 17th gas cylinders were in place there, but, strangely, were not detected. The gas attack was ordered for 5.45 A.M., the tubes were placed over the parapets, sortie steps provided and passages cut in the wire. But the attack was postponed on account of lack of wind, and the troops remained packed in their trenches all day. There was no artillery fire. As the sun began to set the wind rose, and at 4.30 orders were given to attack at 5 P.M. 6,000 cylinders had been placed, and 30 per cent of these were used.

The Germans lost, in the Ypres fighting of 1915, 860 officers, 34,073 other ranks. This does not include the lightly wounded.

On the 7th June, 1915, the first Zeppelin was destroyed in air combat. Lieut. R.A.J. Warneford, Royal Naval Air Service, chased it near Ghent and dropped 20-lb. bombs on it. The explosion was so near that his plane was overturned and his engine stopped. He was forced to make a landing in enemy territory, yet got his engine re-started and escaped. He received the Victoria Cross.

The Lewis gun weighed 26 lbs and could fire 600 rounds per minute, fed by "pans" containing 47 rounds. The Vickers weighed 28-1/2 lbs., ten pounds more when the jacket was full of water, and had a 20-lb. tripod. It used a belt of 250 rounds, but could not fire more than 500 rounds per minute. The arguments about which was best should, I think, be in favour of the Lewis-if considered as a battle weapon.

Inventors were busy during the war. An American invented a giant hose which was to flood the German dugouts-if water enough could be supplied. A steel "crocodile" was built which find its own way forward through brush or entanglements." It worked well-on a parade ground. A chain shot was devised that would drop bombs on a machine gun emplacement; a fan to repel gas clouds; a grapnel that could be shot over the enemy wire-then used to drag the barrier away; a boomerang grenade; a grenade machine like a music box-turn the crank and they shot out, a stream of disc grenades, which ignited like matches against a roughened surface as they flew out; an acetylene gun which dropped shells at short ranges with extraordinary accuracy, but had such delicate mechanism it was useless in the exposure and mud of the front.

Authorization of a pigeon service was asked for in August, 1915. In 1918 20,000 birds were in use, in charge of 380 experts, and 90,000 men trained as fliers.

When Hooge was mined in July, 1915, a gallery 190 feet long was dug, then the 3,500 lbs: of ammonal had to be placed in a chamber above the level of the gallery, which was 6 inches deep in water.

In 1918 one-third of the Royal Air Force fliers in action were Canadians. No other four fliers in the Allied forces made records that could equal those of Canada's four best. They accounted for 230 enemy planes. The best four German fliers, with vastly better machines, had a record of 246 enemy planes-and that is accepting their own figures.

A French soldier deserted on August lst and carried full details of the September 15th, 1915 attack to the enemy. Then a second deserted on the 24th and confirmed all the information of the first.

The first British gas used had a curious effect on the enemy. It caused many of the soldiers a total loss of memory for the day.

At Loos there were only 11,484 Mills bombs available, and these were issued to the Guards.

At Loos the Colonel of the 10th Green Howards rose up and shouted "Charge," and was killed. His second-in-command did the same a moment later. Then the next officer met the same fate, and within five minutes a fourth senior officer had died in exactly the same manner.

At Sanctuary Wood, between June 2nd and 14th, inclusive, the Canadians had 73 officers killed, 257 wounded, 1,053 other ranks killed, 5,010 wounded. In that same time the opposing Germans lost 32 officers killed, 71 wounded, 1,191 other ranks killed, 3,911 wounded. The German excuse for losing what they gained was "a greatly superior artillery," while the truth was that on June 13th they had 40 up-to-strength batteries against 28 British and Canadian ones.

The British Government paid in "claims of war damage" to the French a total of 29,724,573 francs, over a million sterling at the exchange of those days.

From *The Listening Post:*

"FROM THE SHANGHAI FRONT, by our Special Correspondent, See Ah See.

"Expensive Sir-Many things occur in this little war that remind this miserable contributor of the honorable Great War. The magnificent company which your debased scribe disgraces is under the fierce domination of Sergt.-Major Ten Shun, who is possessed of ten thousand devils.

This morning before the break of day he insulted me on parade for having a dirty umbrella. In a voice of thunder he asked me if I knew his honorable mother, and I replied, trembling, that I had not experienced that exquisite pleasure.

Ten Shun then said: "O hideous, unshaven and slovenly private, whose buttons are as bright as the green slime that oozes from the bed of the Yangtse River, it will not be long before you make the unpleasant and regrettable acquaintance with her repulsive son."

Since then I have made that acquaintance, and as one who served in a valiant Chinese Labor Corps in France, the degraded being who presumes to address your higher and more exalted intelligence would say, in the words of the Occidental philosophers, he is acquainted with his honorable onions.

Yesterday honorable company was marching out to fire musketry course. We met

another company marching back, and both companies began to sing to the music of
the band, "Chopsticks-and the same to you." Another song greatly in favor with the
troops is. "If the sergeant steals your rice, never mind."

Here are a few other which I enclose for your unutterable delight :

"Take me back to dear old Foochow;
 Put me on a train for Wei-Hai-Wei.
    Take me right along
    To Canton or Hong Kong,
 Peking, Nanking, Wu Ching-Something.
    Kwang Tung Wong.
Me takee see some nice girl
Far away from Shanghai by the sea.
    Hi tiddley hi ti,
    Japanese me no likee,
Foochow is the place for me."

"Honorable Miss from Ti-ent-sen Pak ah pu,
Honorable Miss from Ti-ent-sen Pak ah pu,
Honorable Miss from Ti-ent-sen
Welly good flend to Chinamen,
    Chinky Pinky Pak ah pu."

May the blossoms of heaven bloom forever on your august grave.-See Ah See."

"What did you see out there, my lad,
That has set that look in your eyes?
    You went out a boy, you have come back a man,
    With strange new depths underneath your tan.
What was it you saw out there, my lad,
That set such depths in your eyes?"

"Strange things-and sad-and wonderful.
    Things that I scarce can tell
I have been in the sweep of the Reaper's scythe-
    With God-and Christ- and hell."

Of all the haunting memories that grip the veteran, remembrance of the long agony
of Pasachendaele usually rules supreme. A stark sea of slime and human debris,
where one saw, smelt, and tasted death; its tragedies burned pictures into the brain of
every survivor who wallowed back to safety. Fifteen years later these pictures have
not dimmed for certain tired-eyed men one meets in the background.

Jock Brown is one of those tired-eyed men. He draws his artificial leg when walking so that his boot makes a rasping noise on the pavement, and sometimes people shrug as they pass by; he makes them nervous. I wish they knew his story.

His company was making an advance at Passchendaele. In the dripping, bone-chilling dawn they had left a line of connected shell holes and plunged through the soupy morass in order to flank a wanted pillbox. There was no barrage worth the mention, and visibility was poor. Sections became divided as they skirted the deeper quagmires. Men became engulfed in the mud and had to be extricated. Others halted through sheer weariness. Yet the company pressed on and in stinking gullies and indescribable places waged fantastic battle with the enemy. One platoon captured a machine gun crew as the men were too exhausted to fight. The prisoners did not know where their comrades were and had not received rations for two days. Fifty yards on were other nests in the mud, but Jock and two others plunged by them in the clinging mist and were suddenly overwhelmed by a shower of stick bombs hurled by a determined party of Germans. The two with Jock were wounded, and the trio surrendered.

The others of his company, at their objective, lay in the filth all day, shivering, almost numbed, too weary to think. Just before dark word came that there was to be a further advance on the left, and the new line was to move forward in order to prevent a gap. There was a moment of bombing as an enemy post resisted, when the victors saw two wounded Germans sprawled in the mud with two dead beside them. Someone called in English, and they saw Jock Brown, his face crusted with blood, his hair matted with it, wedged into a pocket-like cutting beside a dark pool. "Watch your step," he croaked."Don't fall into that water hole."

They tugged Jock from the cavity. He had a bad scalp wound and his face was battered."What hit you, Jock?" they asked him.

He seemed to catch his breath as he answered; "A fist."

"One of those guys?" They pointed at the quartette in field gray.

"No," grunted Jock."Not them. "That was all he would say then, and he stared at the water- filled crater which drained the post until they were relieved.

Back in billets Jock had such a nightmare that his chum woke him, and they sat up in their blankets to have a smoke. It was then Jock told his story.

"We were floundering in the mist, and the next instant a big Heinie had his bayonet against my stomach. I shoved my hands up before I knew what I was doing, but Bell and Jenkins (the two men with him) didn't move fast enough to suit the officer in charge, and he shot both of them. They were severely wounded. The big Heinie and another grabbed me and searched my pockets, then shoved me into that mud hole. Four of the Heinies were ordinary fellows, but the fifth one was a big, ox-like man with a wooden face.

Bell was suffering terribly. The officer had shot him in the stomach. He began to moan and call for help. That German officer was the worst, most cruel-looking person I have ever seen. He shot Bell five times with his automatic. About an hour later Jenkins tried to crawl away. He'd had a bullet through the hip. The officer gave an order to his men. They looked at each other, then put up their rifles and each had a shot at Jenkins. The big man was the only man who didn't put a bullet into him. His shot spattered into the mud beside him, and the officer saw it. He stepped over and slapped the big man in the face. I said something out loud before I thought; and the brute came over and smashed me on the head with his Luger. I guess I was unconscious, or nearly so, because I couldn't help myself though the devil jumped on me with his knees and wedged me down in that hole and pounded me in the face. I guess I was 'out' for a couple of hours, and I was pretty sick when I did `come around.'

The first thing I saw was the officer standing by the big fellow and berating him about something. Then my head was hurting so that I groaned in spite of myself. With that the officer came over, caught me by the feet and tried to pull me into the water. He couldn't do it quickly, so he pointed at the pool and gave the big man an order. I knew what he meant. I was to be drowned in the scum. The big man stood and looked at me, and said something. The officer snarled-and shot him in one leg.

He had his lips back from his teeth so that he looked like an animal, and he pointed at me again. The big fellow shook his head. Crack! It was a bullet in the other leg, and the big man crumpled. But as he went down he reached out and caught the officer by the wrist. They piled into the mud together, and he handled the lieutenant as if he were a child. But he wasn't quite quick enough. The officer had got his `gun' hand free, and his third shot went into the big man's heart-just as he rolled.

He probably died as he made that move, but it was enough. He dropped into the crater with the officer held in his arms, underneath him. There was a string of bubbles from the pool, and that was all. The other four sat and stared at the slime. They never looked at me. And that's the way we were until you fellows came. But every time I shut my eyes I see the face of that officer as he went into the water. It was frightful."

Jock lost his leg in the Amiens show, but he has never lost that Passchendaele horror. I think of him when I hear some of these sleek old boys who were yelling their heads off and blowing whistles and arranging welcomes in '19 say, "Aren't you ever going to forget the war?"

Most of the boys wish they could.

THE ROADS OF MEMORY

"They reach when we are dreaming, alluring, mystic, far;
    They lead to hours, crowded, that knew men as they are.
They stretch from fated Ypres, with all its unseen host,
    Far beyond the slimy Somme, to every `listening post.'
Arras lanes and Bourlon ways, the broken streets of Lens.
    Chalky cuts on Vimy's crest, and dreary Flemish fens.
Beck'ning in the misty gloom, shell-wrecked, ghost-haunted trails,
    The flash of guns their beacon, and their voices bullet wails.

Glow of dawn was never seen by those who travelled there,
    The dark of moon and midnight murk their allocated share;
No plaudits cheered them onward, the roads were rough and long,

They left behind all comfort, all love and light and song.
They asked no meed or mention, and none can name their due;
    They fell, broken in body, or `kept their rendezvous.'
They gained a cross in Flanders; flowers their vigil keep,
    And every cross within those fields some heart has branded deep.
Some roads were cobbled highways and some were duckwalks crude;
    Death whispered over all them, nor softened in his brood.
Each plodder felt his presence, nearer with every mile,
    Yet no man there turned backward, but faced him with a smile.
Their choice had been to battle, to serve another's need-
    More than a million doctrines lost in a single creed.
There were more envies shattered, more friendships had their birth,
    More mothers' prayers remembered there than any place on earth.

These roads we only picture as far we could see,
    Yet know they wended onward to where Time cannot be;
Where bayonets and rifles and shells are never known,
    We'll see the roadway's ending when our Last Post has blown.
Till then those travellers honor, their Faith, their Hope, their Aim,
    And bid those coming after never forget their Name.
Whene'er that Legion passes, are those who feel its breath-
    The men who marched to battle and with them looked at death."

"It was dark at last. The first flare lights went up, sizzling in a long rush and flooding the parapet with light. And as the wavering whitish glow descended all the stakes and stubs in No Man's Land seemed moving shadows. It was very still; only an occasional gun was firing over on our left near Hill 70.

"Jimmy was on the fire-step, looking over. The ration party had gone, and there were no extra duties for us. It was warm enough, and we could smell the flowers and tree blossoms in the ruined French garden behind the trench. The officer came along, our platoon commander. It wasn't his "turn" on, but he often came that way. He sat down with Tom and me and talked about fishing up the rivers in New Brunswick. And when Jimmy stood down and I took the trick they told each other about some new-fangled flies they'd used. They must have been talking there a couple of hours. It helped make the time go, and, somehow, I never forgot nights like that. It was so quiet-like, with the flares dropping like a white `hush,' and their voices, low and so eager and chummy. Say, he was a fine officer. When I think of them times I wish. . . ,"

From "Our Lieutenant."

THE END.

William Richard Bird
1891-1984

Will Bird was born in Mapleton, Nova Scotia, May 11, 1891. He was the first son of Stephen Bird, by his second wife, Augusta (nee Bird), of Amherst, Nova Scotia. He was preceded by his two half-brothers, Harry (1885) and Hubert (1886), from his father's first wife. In 1893 a fourth Bird brother, Lew, was born.

In December 1895, with Augusta 4 months pregnant, tragedy struck the family when their father, Stephen died suddenly. Five months after Stephen Bird's death, Augusta gave birth to another son, a namesake for her late husband, Stephen Carmen. Later that year Augusta Bird moved back to her hometown of Amherst bringing with her the 5 year old Will, Lew, the baby Stephen and the two sons from the late Stephen's previous marriage, Hubert and Harry.

The younger boys were educated in Amherst, at the High School and later Stephen went to work for the Canada Car Company. Both Will and Stephen competed in athletics, were keen baseball players and "red-hot" fans of both baseball and hockey. The two were very close, shared mutual likes and dislikes and "could read each other's minds".

With the outbreak of war in 1914, Stephen enlisted as a Corporal in the 25th Nova Scotia Battalion. Will also rushed to join the Colours but Stephen, using his influence, had Will turned down. Disheartened Will went to the Prairies to farm. In May 1915 the 25th Battalion sailed for England.

The 25th Battalion went to France in mid-September 1915 and occupied trenches at Kemmel, just south of Ypres, Belgium. On September 25th the inexperienced men of the 25th suffered their first fatality. Just before 5 pm on October 8, 1915 the Germans blew a large, underground explosive charge beneath the 25th's frontline trenches. The explosion created a hole 65 feet by 35 feet and 25 feet deep. It had killed 2 men outright, wounded 20, and 10 men were listed as "missing".

That same October found Will bringing in the harvest on a small farm in Saskatchewan, pitching sheaves into a wagon, when Stephen walked out from behind a farmcart ! They did not speak and soon Stephen vanished. Three days later Will received official notification that Stephen Bird, was missing, presumed dead in the mine explosion. His body was never found.

The well-liked Stephen had been popular amongst his comrades and one wrote to the Bird family after his death; "He had splendid courage and when urged to fall back a little further a few minutes before the explosion his reply was 'I am staying right here' ".

Another wrote "He was a friend at all times and under all circumstances, no one need wish a better friend, we all loved him and we all mourn his loss". No one mourned his loss more than Will.

Will returned to Amherst and in April 1916 enlisted in the 193rd Battalion, Nova Scotia Highlanders. The 193rd Battalion was a locally-raised battalion and the men who comprised its ranks were all from the area and included Hubert Bird, Will's half brother. (The number block allocated to the 193rd Nova Scotia Highlanders was 901001 to 904000, Will Bird's service number was 901552).

In October 1916 the 193rd sailed for England. Upon arrival it was broken up for reinforcements and Will Bird and a number of his friends were shipped to France to reinforce the 42nd Battalion, The Black Watch of Canada, in the frontline. On January 5, 1917 the men from Nova Scotia joined the kilted Montrealers in the trenches in front of the infamous Vimy Ridge.

The 42nd had served in France since 1915 and had fought in the major battles of Mount Sorrel and the Somme when Will joined them in late 1916. Throughout the war the Black Watch fought with exceptional ferocity and success. By the end of the war 800 men had been killed and 2000 wounded of the 6000 men who passed through the ranks of the battalion. Shortages of reinforcements from Montreal brought many men from across Canada into their ranks and this is how Will Bird ended up with the Montrealers.

Will Bird served with the 42nd Battalion throughout the war until demobilized back in Canada in March 1919. He was awarded a Military Medal for bravery in the capture of Mons, on the night of 10-11 November 1918, the last night of the war.

Will returned to Southampton, Nova Scotia and in 1919, married Ethel Sutton, his childhood sweetheart and had 2 children, Stephen Stanley in 1920 and Betty in 1923. The family moved to Amherst in 1923 and later to Halifax.

Like many veterans Will did not know which way to go after the war but through some good fortune and good writing found a career in journalism. During the 1930's his First World War memoir "And We Go On" was published, followed by a series of articles on visiting the old battlefields for Macleans magazine. The two publications brought Will into prominence in the burgeoning remembrance movement brought about by the aging veterans in the 1930's.

Will Bird was a prolific writer on many topics: fiction, non-fiction, books, magazines, articles, newspapers, columns and short stories. Over the years he became a literary presence in his native Nova Scotia.

The years took a toll on the many who survived the war. In 1939, Will's half brother Hubert, who had lost a leg at the Drocourt-Queant line, died. But the hardest blow came in 1944 when his son, Stephen was killed in Normandy. He was 24. Captain Stephen Stanley Bird of the North Nova Scotia Highlanders was killed in action July 8, 1944. He is buried in Beny-sur-Mer Canadian War Cemetery, France. Will often blamed his writing about his war experiences as a factor in his son's rush to enlist.

The road continued to take its toll and in 1977 his half brother, Harry died and in 1982, his beloved Ethel passed away. Will followed her in 1984.

Will Bird is survived by his daughter, Betty Murray, of Amherst and 4 grandchildren. Stephen McKay Murray carries on the name and will never have to suffer the fate of his namesakes.